FALLING FROM THE NEST

Falling From The Nest

JAN ELLIS

Jan Ellis

For Mother

To my sister, Diana Van Rossum - Thanks
Without her help this book wouldn't exist

Thanks to the members of the RRWG for their critiques
and encouragement, especially
Kathrine Latham, Jerry Stratton, and James Goolsby

Special thanks to my wonderful, patient editor,
Brandon Beck

REVIEWS

Ellis's debut novel is a riveting memoir about growing into truth and love – not just of others but of self. Sometimes, a young girl learns too young that the world teaches hate more quickly than it teaches love. Sometimes a young girl sees love in those very places where the world tries so very hard to kill beauty and light. She holds on tight to what she sees and draws it out and amplifies it. Jan Ellis grew up in Minnesota in the 40s and 50s with a father who was told, and believed, that her mother was crazy. He sent her mother away and worried that Jan was so much like her mother she may have inherited the "crazy" gene. Yet Jan saw the truth, beauty, and love in her mother, and, finally, maybe even just a little in her father after 80 years. Ellis's stories of women and mental health care (or lack thereof) throughout her life from the perspective of the person whose mother was kept from her, captivate and educate. This book reveals truths, that in their beauty, break open secrets that shine needed light into gaps in our country's history around patriarchy and healthcare.

I love memoir for the potential the genre has for the audience to see themselves as not alone for the first time – especially in a way that has been a part of a family secret or shame. In bibliotherapy, one of the practices I use in mental health chaplaincy is guided book discussions, encouraging self-reflective healing. Rarely do I find a book for people who remember the carceral nature of the US psychiatric facilities of the early-mid twentieth century. The perspective of the children of the residents is even rarer, and, yet, deserves just as much attention, if not more. Family systems theory demands it. *Falling from the Nest* will be a part of my chaplaincy practice from now on. Jan's poignant and clear stories, complete with research-based endnotes accompaniment, create

a point from which others can begin to feel whole in their own, similar experiences.
BRANDON JONNA BECK, chaplain and educator

The story was riveting and well written. It was a wonderful and easy read. I wished it was longer so I could experience more of the world Jan revealed. I went through the emotional rollercoaster of the events in her life and liked the fusion of humor and the daily real life mess. The book is rich with wisdom, documenting a part of our history and how we treat each other, as seen through a child's, then young adult's, eyes. I could say a lot more because there is so much in it. Despite being interrupted by a tornado slamming into my house, I'm very glad I lived through the tornado so I could finish this book.
SANTIAGO SATORI author of *Finding You*

CONTENTS

1	Les and Millie, Their Stories	1
2	Mr. Bow Tie	7
3	Running Away	9
4	Sunday Dinners	11
5	Happy Days	15
6	Down Hill	19
7	The Lobotomy	21
8	Mother's Letter	25
9	Anna	31
10	New Normal	33

11	Next New Normal	35
12	No Great Christmas After All	39
13	Billy	47
14	Summer Camp	49
15	The Nutgoodie	55
16	The Revival	59
17	Home Again	61
18	The Golden Rule	63
19	Who's Your Mama?	65
20	Rene	69
21	Babe	73
22	The Family Car	75
23	Mother's Teeth	77

24	"Please Release Me, Let Me Go"	79
25	Bambi's Child	83
26	Show and Tell	87
27	Show and Tell II	89
28	Body Image	91
29	On Being Frank	93
30	"Paul Said ...."	97
31	Stories from Seventh Grade	101
32	Chow Mein	107
33	Chartreuse	111
34	Cars	113
35	Irene's Story	115
36	Dad's Divorce	119

37	Jim	121
38	The Runaway	123
39	Jim Returns	129
40	The Transom	133
41	My Blue Bathing Suit	137
42	Looking For Sailors	139
43	Kay's Wedding Dress	141
44	Judy	143
45	Jerry	145
46	Illegitimate	147
47	A New Start	153
48	Free At Last - Sort Of	157
49	Betty and Tyler	159

50	Road Trip	163
51	Settling In	165
52	Not a Dog	169
53	Mother's Visits	173
54	Clarence for the Last Time	175
55	Jerry for the Last Time	177
56	Mother	179
57	Dad	181
58	Life Goes On	185
59	The Three-Legged Frog - A Fairytale	187

Notes and References   191

| 1 |

Les and Millie, Their Stories

These are my parents, Les Druley and Millie McGee. They were both born in 1914.

Millie HS graduation

Millie's parents were first generation immigrants; Grandpa (Walter McGee) came from Scotland when he was six, the youngest of eleven. His father was a baker but when he tried to form a baker's union, he was blackballed and had to find a new profession. Walter quit school after the third grade to get a job and help the family. Grandma (Alida) emigrated from Norway at sixteen and found work as a maid.

Walter said, "The minute I saw Alida, I knew I was going to marry her."

He would sing "Waltzing Matilda" to her (Alida's middle name). Together they raised seven children and seemed to love every minute of it. Alida made the rules and everyone lived by them, including Walter, who gladly behaved like one of the kids. The summer when Millie was four and Walter was shaving the boys' heads (to prevent lice), Millie wanted her head shaved, "like the boys."

When Alida came home from the store, she cried, "What have you done to my beautiful baby's curls?"

Millie played baseball, tennis, and street games with her brothers, Don and Fred and she was known as Lefty or Shorty (when she was fully grown, she was less than five feet tall and left-handed). Sometimes, if the kids were bored, they'd go to the train yard and hop trains. They were all regulars at church. According to Don, the minister begged them to join a different church because they were so rowdy.

Walter made his living selling life insurance. He would go door to door collecting a nickel every week from each of his clients. Sometimes he'd keep the nickel when money was tight. One of his customers had avoided him for several weeks so he took the chair from his porch as payment. That chair stayed in the family long after Walter was gone. Walter was adamant that all his children needed to graduate from high school and all seven, except Ethel, did. Alida gave everyone a chore. Irene's was making clothes for the family; Don's was keeping the floors clean; Millie's was ironing. She loved to iron. They were all close, and they'd all meet regularly for picnics and birthdays and Sunday dinners. There was always a heated discourse about politics, music, or religion. As soon as they were bored with one topic, someone would bring up something new to argue about.

Les HS graduation

The Druleys were much different family. The family had been Americans for many generations and can be traced back to the Mayflower. Before Les's generation, the men were college educated, and married college educated women. My great-grandfather (Leslie) was a successful owner of several granaries and known to be miserly. Leslie had three children, Lisle, Helen, and Collis. When Helen was born they couldn't agree on a name so until she was twelve she was called by several different names. At twelve, she was told she could pick her own name and she chose Helen. Leslie promised Helen the lot next to his home when she graduated from college, but, when she asked for it, he sold it and kept the money.

"It's my property and I can do whatever I want with it," he told Helen.

My grandfather (Lisle) graduated from Macalester College in St. Paul with a degree in chemistry and took a job selling farm equipment. He married grandmother (Vera Tormey) although his parents didn't think she was a good fit for their family. She was a first-generation immigrant from Ireland. Lisle was verbally abusive to Vera and to Les (the oldest of their five children). More than once Dad (Les) said, "I try not to be like my father," referring to the constant verbal abuses, but he fell short.

Lisle invented an artificial rubber and patented it. During the First World War, when there was a rubber shortage, Lisle donated his patent to the war effort as an act of patriotism, never to be used by the government. Lisle used his artificial rubber to make and sell fishing lures during the Great Depression though. His best seller was Minny the Swimmer.

As the Depression progressed, Lisle's farm equipment sales dwindled, and he borrowed against all the furniture in order to pay rent. Then he lost his job entirely. That same year, Vera died of uremic poisoning. Their twelve-year-old, youngest son, William, died of a burst appendix two months later. Then Vera's mother died.

This was also the year Les graduated from high school as Valedictorian and Class President. Lisle lost the furniture and couldn't pay the rent so he took three of his remaining children and moved to Prescott, Wisconsin, leaving Les behind to work off their debts at the grocery store, butcher, and the bank. Les lived in a tent behind the grocery store and bagged groceries until he paid off all the bills. After the family debts were paid off, Les and his tent went to work for the CCC (Civilian Conservation Corps) to earn money for his family. He went on to earn an associate degree in business. During that time, Les met Millie and her family. Millie's brother, Pat, and Les opened a driving range. When that wasn't successful, they became house painters. Pat stayed with it and eventually got a job in maintenance at the University of Minnesota where he stayed until he retired. Les didn't like working on a ladder.

1936

When they were both twenty-three years old, and after he graduated with an associate degree in business, Les and Millie married. Les went to work for his grandfather's granary in Ellendale, Minnesota to be the manager/bookkeeper but when he got there, he just unloaded bags of grain and wasn't paid enough to support him and Millie. Millie went back home to Minneapolis to have their first child, Diana. Millie worked for the telephone company and hid her marriage and pregnancy as long as she could because the telephone company would not allow married women to work for them.
Les got a job as a machinist in Minneapolis, and they moved into a state housing project near downtown. Both I and my sister, Linda, were born in the "projects."
As soon as Les saved enough, he bought a beer parlor named The Mug with a two-bedroom apartment upstairs, and we moved out of the

housing project into our new home. The rent paid by Jim, the proprietor of The Mug, was enough to pay the mortgage.

And they lived happily ever after????

Our home above The Mug

| 2 |

Mr. Bow Tie

I met Mr. Bow Tie, in the fall, when I was three.

me and Diana

I was anxiously waiting for Diana to return from school (she was in the first grade), so Mother said I could go around to the front of The Mug and wait for her on the sidewalk.

A man walked up to me as I stood on the sidewalk and said, "Hello. What's your name, little girl?"

"Janice. What's yours?"

"You can call me Mr. Bow Tie. Do you like candy, Janice? I'm walking over there to the grocery store, and, if you want to keep me company, I'll buy you whatever kind of candy you like. How does that sound?"

The store was down at the other end of the block and across the street.

"I'm not allowed to cross the street without my mother."

"Well then, I can buy you candy at the drugstore on the corner."

So, I took his hand and went with him. In the drugstore, I went straight to the counter to pick out my candy while he went directly to the back of the drug store.

He said, "Come here, Janice. I want to show you something."

He pulled a curtain aside and there was Ned, the druggist's bedroom! I didn't know Ned lived in the drugstore.

"Come on in."

"No."

I couldn't think of any reason I would be interested in a closer look at Ned's bedroom. It was kind of dark and messy and a little scary. Besides, I was much more interested in picking out my candy. I went back to the candy counter, showed Ned the candy I wanted, and waited for Mr. Bow Tie to pay for it.

"Thank you, Mr. Bow Tie."

And I hurried back to my spot on the sidewalk to wait for Diana. I shared my candy and told her my new friend, Mr. Bow Tie, bought it for me.

When we told Mother about the wonderful man who bought me candy, she sat Diana and me down to explain a new rule.

"Never, never, ever go off with a stranger."

"But Mr. Bow Tie isn't a stranger. He's my friend."

"Never go off with anyone, even if we all know them, unless you ask me first, and I say it's okay. And even if they say I told them it was okay, you need to hear it from me. So, what do you say if someone wants you to go with them?"

"I have to ask my mother," we said in unison.

The next time I saw Mr. Bow Tie coming down the street, he crossed to the other side. I thought he must not have seen me, so I waved and called to him, "Hi, Mr. Bow Tie."

"I can't talk to you anymore. If I do, I'll go to jail," he called back, and hurried on his way.

| 3 |

Running Away

"Can I go out and play?" I asked Mother.

"No. Linda will be waking up soon from her nap, and I want you to entertain her while I sew."

"Then I'm going to run away!"

Mistakenly I thought the world revolved around me and I was sure she would do anything to keep me.

Instead, Mother stopped sewing and said, "You better take a change of clothes. You can tie them in a hanky and carry them on the end of a stick. Oh, where will you eat dinner? Maybe you should take some food, too."

She seemed happy to help me plan my runaway! I had to think about this. If she was really going to let me go, I had to have a plan. I decided the only clothes I really needed to take was my pretty, ruffled sunsuit, but it was in the top of the closet, and I couldn't reach it, even standing on a chair.

"I need my sun suit, but I can't reach it. Can you get it down for me?"

She just sat there at the sewing machine with an almost-smile and said, "If you're running away, you need to learn to do things for yourself. I won't be there to help you."

"I'll need some sandwiches and a banana and an orange and a bottle of milk."

"I can't let you take the milk. It's the only bottle we have, and we don't have any bananas. Besides, all that will be heavy and a lot to carry while running away. Oh, and you better take your pillow and a blanket. It gets pretty cold out there at night"

There was that almost-smile again. No sunsuit, no milk, and no banana. And how could I play if I had to drag around my pillow and a blanket? Maybe I didn't want to run away after all.

"Okay, I'll stay and play with Linda," I heavily sighed. Mother went back to sewing.

Besides, I liked playing with Linda. Next time I decide to run away, I'll have a better reason and a plan.

| 4 |

Sunday Dinners

When we moved above the Mug, our new home was only a couple of blocks from Grandpa and Grandma McGee. Almost every Sunday we walked from church to their home for Sunday dinner. There were always plenty of aunts and uncles and cousins there, too. Mother and my aunts spent the afternoon in the kitchen with Grandma, fixing dinner and washing dishes while laughing and gossiping. Dad, Grandpa, and my uncles sat in the living room with the curtains closed, smoking cigars, and listening to classical music while arguing politics, religion, music, and anything else they could think of to disagree on. When Uncle Pat and Uncle Fred were released from the Army, Uncle Pat used the money he saved while in the army to buy the latest in Hi Fi equipment. The only thing everyone agreed on was the wonderful sound coming out of Pat's Hi Fi. He used his GI bill money to take painting classes at the Walker Art School. Sometimes I'd just sit on the dining room floor and draw. Pat would look at my drawings and say my drawings were amazing and I was a great artist. I believed him.

We all looked forward to Sunday. Us cousins either went outside to play, played on the dining room floor, or played hide-and-seek all over the house. Grandma kept a small toy upholstered chair (I think it was supposed to be a pin-cushion) on the floor in the dining room closet. The seat lifted and inside it was full of little glass animals and other knick knacks, mostly broken. I liked to play with the glass dog, holding its broken leg where it should have been so it could run around the room barking. Of course, we had to be a little quiet so as not to disturb the music playing loudly in the living room, which wasn't hard to do.

One time, when we were playing hide-and-seek upstairs, Diana opened the floor vent in Fred's bedroom so we could secretly spy on the men in the living room. A shower of a thousand toenails fell on Grandpa.

"What the hell?"

Apparently Fred clipped his toenails into the floor vent so he wouldn't have to pick them up. He just didn't intend to open the vent.

When I was in Kindergarten, Grandpa asked me what I was learning in school.

"I'm learning to tell time," I said proudly.

"That's easy. I'll teach you how to tell time right now."

He proceeded to talk about fifteen and thirty and quarters and three quarters and noon and half and sixty. My mind was spinning as I tried to remember where all these new things were on the clock without having a clue what any of them had to do with telling time. Mother was listening. She was smiling in anticipation of how this would end.

Grandpa said, "Okay, when the big hand is on twelve and the little hand is on three, what time is it?"

"A quarter?"

I could tell right away by Grandpa's look that I guessed wrong. Before he could say anything, I said, "No, wait. It's thirty."

Grandpa threw up his hands and said, "I can't teach you to tell time. You're too stupid."

Mother no longer looked amused. "Janice is not stupid! You're the one who's stupid. You couldn't even teach a five-year-old to tell time, for Christ's sake."

Grandpa looked at me and said, "Your mother's right. I'm the stupid one."

We all went back to other things, Grandpa to his music, Mother to the kitchen, and me to the little glass dog.

Still, I was anxious to get back to school and finish learning to tell time, just to prove Mother was right that I wasn't stupid.

| 5 |

Happy Days

Recently I found my report card from first grade in an old box of pictures. The teacher wrote, *Janice is a good student but can't be rushed, which is probably why she is late to school so often.*

I remember my early school days well. I walked to school with my best friend, Wayne. Our chosen route took us down alleys and over fences. Of course, once we climbed over a fence, we had to sneak through the yard to get out the gate on the other side without being seen.

Wayne's grandmother had turned her home into a boarding house, and it happened to be next to one of the alleys on our route to school. All of her tenants were very old, and most could hardly move. Wayne's grandma gave us milk and cookies, but first we had to come in and greet all the tenants. They absolutely loved us and looked forward to our visits, so much so that if anyone wasn't present when we got there, we'd have to wait for them to get to the living room to talk to us. After our report cards arrived, Wayne's grandma said we couldn't come in anymore – we needed to get to school.

I lived on the south side of our block, and Wayne lived on the west side. After school and on weekends, we roamed our alley looking for things to do. Our alley was H-shaped, so we had lots of territory to cover.

When people were in their yard, we'd ask what they were doing. If they were gardening, we'd offer to "help." If they were just drinking lemonade and eating cookies, we'd join them. Wayne's next-door neighbor (on the left side of his house) was crabby and told him to stay out of her yard. So, we'd sneak over her fence and pee in her yard. I did it once, but it was too much of a bother, what with having to pull down my pants and getting pee on my shoes and having no toilet paper. But I was happy to continue to sneak into the yard with Wayne so he could pee.

Linda, Wayne, and me

There was a butcher shop on the north side of our block. We started going in there whenever we saw the shop was busy and would play in the sawdust. It was great for sliding and making roads and throwing. We'd leave before the last customer left. It only took a few visits before the butcher figured out we weren't with any of his customers and he told us not to come back.

Wayne's mother let us take furniture and blankets into the yard to build forts. We'd have several rooms by the end of the day and she'd bring our lunch to us in the fort.

Once, we found a metal coffee lid and were sailing it around when it hit Wayne's next door neighbor in the head (the neighbor to the right of his house – not the crabby neighbor to the left). She had to go to the hospital for stitches and her whole head was in a bandage. We got a 'looong' lecture from Wayne's mother and had to go and apologize – and listen to another 'looong' lecture from the lady's husband.

He said, "You kids could have killed her! You should be spanked."

That sounded like a terrible idea. After that, we paid more attention to where we threw things.

Next door to my home above The Mug was a welding shop where they made swing sets. They would let Wayne and me in the shop to "test" the finished swing sets before they were painted. Alas, that came to a stop when we started "testing" the freshly painted sets put out overnight in the shop yard to dry. The shop yard was surrounded by a chain-link fence and locked, but we could squeeze through the gate. Mother wasn't happy about the red paint all over my hands and clothes either. And we weren't allowed into the shop to test the sets any more.

That Fall, Mother bought me a brown snowsuit.

I said, "I'm not wearing that! It's ugly and brown."

"Yes, you WILL wear it. In fact, I'm going to buy you a brown snowsuit every year until you learn to stay clean."

Diana in her red snowsuit and me in my brown one

I hated to think I'd have to wear brown snow suits for the rest of my life. Getting my clothes dirty came with playing outside. I couldn't help that.

These are the cherished memories of my happy childhood when I was confident of my place in my family and even the whole world. None of us were prepared for the dramatic changes ahead.

| 6 |

Down Hill

August 7, 1947 - My brother, Steve, was born. As fortune would have it, Diana, Linda, and I had the measles. It was decided that the best thing to do was to leave Steve in the hospital and let Mother come home to take care of us. She became sad, overwhelmed, and anxious. Dad and Mother consulted Mother's doctor, Dr. Bacon.

Dr. Bacon said, "The best thing to do is to leave her alone. The faster she resumes her role as mother and wife, the faster she will recover. Helping her with her responsibilities will only delay her recovery."

I don't know how long Steve stayed in the hospital, but by the time he was able to come home, Mother was angry. Dad worked nights and slept during the day in the attic. He'd come down yelling at Mother because Steve's crying was waking him up.

Our normal routines were beginning to crack. Several times, Diana went back to school late after lunch crying because Mother wouldn't get off the phone to fix her lunch. She was complaining about Dad to whoever would listen. But no one listened.

Now Mother's doctor thought she must have suffered a nervous breakdown. The solution for her nervous breakdown was to put her in a rest home. Our next door neighbor's teenage daughter came over after school to baby-sit when Dad went to work. Mother wasn't getting better and Dad couldn't afford the added expenses so Mother came home after a couple of months in the rest home. She was madder than ever at Dad for sending her away from her family.

Dad told Grandma and Grandpa, "I'm not worried about Millie hurting the kids. She's always been a good mother. I was worried for myself. All her anger is directed at me and she scares me."

In May 1948, when Mother was just thirty-three, Diana was ten, I was seven, Linda was four, and Steve was under one, she was taken to the Mayo Clinic in Rochester Minnesota and given a lobotomy. She didn't want to go.

"I don't need or want an operation to change me. I don't know what the problem is. I still take care of the kids, cook, and clean like I always have. I know I am getting angry a lot since I got home from the hospital but I'm working on it. Don't make me go."

"It's just a small operation to make you calm down. Dr. Bacon thinks it will help," Dad said.

| 7 |

The Lobotomy

Dad took Mother to the hospital alone. We (kids) couldn't ride along. Dad said she'd be home in two weeks. He brought Mother to the hospital and the hospital sent a telegram telling Dad when the surgery was scheduled. No one went to the hospital to be with her. She was alone.

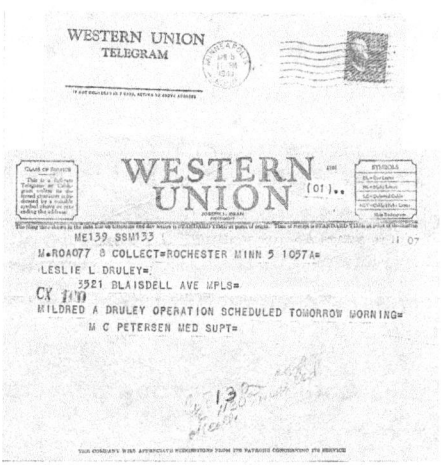

After two weeks in the hospital following her surgery, we all went to pick her up. We were excited to see her and hear all about her surgery. It was a beautiful spring day and Dad told us to wait outside while he went in to get Mother.

In front of the hospital was a big park with a small gazebo in the center and several benches and gliders. We tried everything out but still, it seemed like forever before they finally came out. We were excited to see Mother again.

Mother came out with her whole head in bandages.

"Why is your head in a bandage?" "What did they do in the surgery?" "Did it hurt?" "Do you have a headache?" and on and on until we realized she wasn't answering any of our questions. She just looked at us like she didn't know who we were.

Dad said, "She's just tired."

Mother didn't say anything all the way home. We sat quietly in the back seat trying to figure out what was going on. And once at home, she sat all day in the living room rocking her body back and forth in her chair, smoking and holding Linda on her lap. She still wasn't talking, but after a week or so, she started to listen to her records and sometimes sing along. I could see she was getting better, and we waited patiently for her bandages to be removed. I thought, *when the bandages on her head were removed, she'll be okay.* It was scary to think she forgot who we were so I hovered around the house watching and hoping to see signs that Mother was getting better. I think she was beginning to know who we were.

But, after only two weeks at home, and before her bandages were removed, Dad packed her in the car and drove her back to the hospital in Rochester only this time he took her to the state mental hospital. She didn't object – could she have? But I did.

"Why does she have to go back? She's getting better."

Dad said, "No, your mother isn't getting any better. I need someone here I can trust to take care of you kids."

But the hospital sent her home after about a month, proclaiming her sane.

After the extra month to recuperate, when Mother returned home, she was a lot better. She knew who we were. She mostly talked on the phone and sat and smoked though. Dad would become angry with

Mother's lack of interest in doing anything, she would lash back at him, "I want a divorce!" She couldn't stop. "I want a divorce!"

Dad became angrier and more frustrated trying to reason with her.

"Why isn't dinner ready? I work hard all day and come home to the house in a mess and no dinner on the table. What have you been doing all day?" he would shout.

"Get your own goddam dinner. I want a divorce," Mother shouted back.

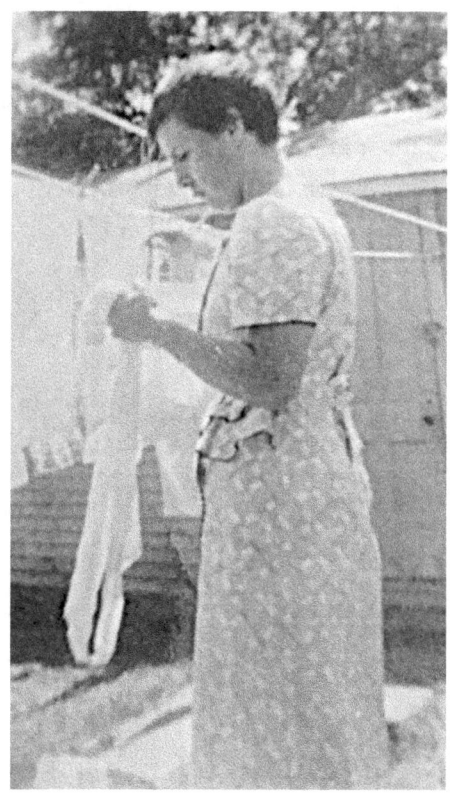

That year, for Christmas, Mother went to Dayton's Department Store and charged Christmas presents for us all. She didn't have time (and probably the ability) to make our presents like she used to do. When Dad found out, he had a fit, returned all the presents, and told Dayton's that Mother was not allowed to charge anything there – ever.

When Christmas arrived that year, it was just a lot of yelling and fighting.

"I want a divorce!"

That was the beginning of many sad, forgettable Christmases.

It wasn't the fighting itself that bothered me. I quickly learned that if I argued with Dad, I could easily be banished to the mental hospital. It broke my heart to hear my mother stand up to my father, knowing what would happen next.

Please, please, be quiet. He'll be gone again in the morning and you'll be able to stay with us.

Right after Christmas, Mother was taken back to Rochester State Mental Hospital.

Dad said, "This time she won't be coming home again."

After Mother's second commitment, Dad hired a housekeeper, Anna Larsen and I knew for sure that Mother was never coming home again. This traumatized Diana so Dad made arrangements with Grandma and Grandpa to let her live with them for a while.

| 8 |

Mother's Letter

After Mother was back in Rochester State Hospital for about a month, she wrote this letter to Dad and us kids.

To my dear Valentines, Mother, with a hug & kiss to each of you. Am I still your Valentine, Les? kisses, Mildred

February 14, 1949 Dearest Les & children, Hope you had a nice birthday party, Janice. Did you celebrate Grandma's birthday, Sunday? There was a million and one things I meant to ask you and discuss when you came but somehow - oh well, next time you pay me a visit will you "kindly" let me know when you're coming? There's enough - or perhaps it best YOU tell me a few things for a change. How's the "weather?" Well, honey, seriously how are you and each of the children? Hope you can come and see me again in the not too distant future. How's about sending me three packages of cigarettes 3 Herbert Tareytons. I ordered some Luckies but won't get them for a couple of weeks and if you didn't leave me some money at the office, the order will be ignored. Forgot to order K. Could use them now and will need them before another order goes in. Oh yes, also send some thumb tacks so I can work on that pillow. Where's that blouse pattern and yarn I've been expecting? I received a heart box of chocolates for Valentines Day. Must write a letter thanking the folks for remembering me. Here's a kiss for each of you for a Valentine. Too bad you didn't come this week end. If you're interested in hearing from me again, please send some stamps and stationery. I must trust the hospital to mail &

stamp this letter if it is to reach you. You're entitled to one letter a week, gratis, so this is it for this week. Did you get a housekeeper to take Ellen's place. Please tell me how everything is. Wish you'd write more often and come down here more often. Six weeks without seeing you is more than I can bear. Wish it were possible to see you every week. I miss you and the children so much that words just can't express it. Please send me a subscription to the Morning Tribune also the Sunday Tribune. Let me know if I have money in the office as I would like to order some ice-cream. Please call the folks and let them know I received the candy as I may not get stamps for a while. Ethel mailed it from Daytons. She and Emile and Irene & Wally and the folks sent it together. Well, dearest, please answer pronto and let me know when you can see me again. Kiss each of the children for me and here's hoping to be with you all soon. Love Mildred (Mother)

For the next fifteen years, the state hospitals sent her home as "cured" another thirteen times. Each time Mother returned home, the fighting began again. And she would never be home long before Dad had her recommitted.

When she was home, she didn't seem to know what to do next. She accomplished little around the house and spent most of her time on the phone, trying to find a lawyer to help her and complaining about Dad to everyone she knew. When she got started on the subject of the many atrocities committed against her at the hospital, she couldn't stop talking about it.

Even her parents and siblings would finally say, "Millie, just shut up! No one wants to hear about that." But I did.

| 9 |

Anna

With Mother gone, Dad hired Anna Larsen as our housekeeper. Anna was a Norwegian immigrant (like Grandma) and had a farm in southern Wisconsin which she gave to her son and his family when her husband died. She decided she was in the way so came to the Twin Cities to look for work.

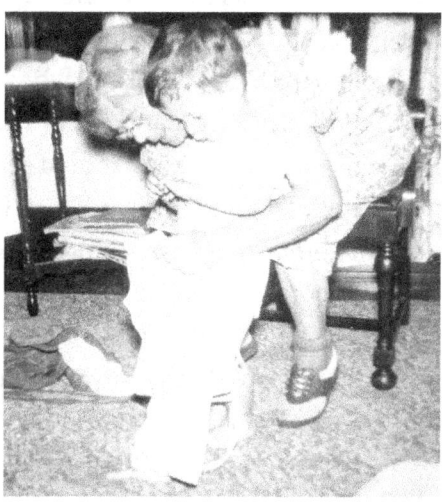

I loved her – she was a lot like Mother in how she treated us and she adored Steve. She called him "Punky."

She used to say to Steve, "Whose little boy are you?"

"Anna's!"

Our little two-bedroom home above the Mug was pretty crowded, I guess. Dad worked nights and slept in the attic during the day. That summer he bought a four-bedroom house in another part of town and suddenly everything changed - again. Now not only did I lose Mother but I lost my best friend, Wayne. Wayne taught me how to spit through the gap in my teeth but too soon the gap disappeared and then even my special gift from Wayne was gone.

At least we still had Anna, and Diana came home once we moved into the new house. Anna treated me like I was almost a grown-up and whenever I said I was hungry, she'd say, "Fix yourself a sandwich."

So, I ate peanut butter sandwiches endlessly until one day Anna said, "Do you know what peanut butter is made of?"

"Peanuts?"

"No, smashed up worms."

I knew she was lying but I still couldn't eat any more peanut butter. So, I switched to sardine sandwiches. Anna showed me how to smear their little faces and bodies on the bread until you couldn't see them anymore. It was gross but better than squished worms.

I noticed beautiful, confident women swung their hips wide and gracefully when they walked, so I decided I should practice walking like that. With each step I took, I'd bend one knee and drop my hip as far as I could, poking out the other hip. It was kind of jerky but I thought, with practice, it would smooth out.

Anna asked, "Yanice (she couldn't pronounce Js), is something wrong? Why are you walking like that? Did you break something?"

I said, "No, this is the way I've always walked."

Finally, I had to give up though. It just took too long to get anywhere.

After a few months in the new house, Anna quit. She was Grandma's age and had diabetes and couldn't manage running up and down the stairs all day.

| 10 |

New Normal

Dad went through the county welfare system to get housekeepers but they didn't stay long. My favorite of these was Rose although she was no Mother or Anna. She was so cheerful and absent-minded. She wanted me in the kitchen whenever she cooked so I could find everything (spoons, pans, potato peelers, etc.) I'd tell her when Steve needed changing or did it myself.

We almost never visited Mother at Rochester State Hospital and most of the times we visited Mother while she was in St. Peter State Hospital was when Mother's family would arrange a family picnic at a park in St. Peter or when she was released and we went to pick her up. The hospital was about sixty miles away, and Dad apparently didn't want to take a day to visit Mother. He was often working two jobs or was taking classes at night school and I guess he wanted Sundays off. He probably wouldn't have gone at all to these picnics if there had been anyone that could have fit the four of us kids in their car with their own family.

While it was fun to get back together with our cousins, we never had time alone with Mother on these visits. Riding there, we were excited and anxious to see Mother and imagined all the things we were going to tell her. The ride home was silent and sad; we thought of all the things we didn't get a chance to say. And Diana usually went to her room to cry when we got back home.

When Mother came home for one of her all too short stays, it was great! One time she took me on the bus to our old neighborhood so I could see Wayne. It was one of the happiest days of my young life. Wayne and I walked arm-in-arm around the block remembering all the great things we did while Mother sat on their porch talking to Wayne's mother. When we got home, Dad yelled at Mother for taking me. And all too soon Mother was snatched away once more and I never saw Wayne again.

| 11 |

Next New Normal

Mother was gone again and Dad was having trouble keeping "housekeepers." Dad found a family of four that would live with him and Steve, and, in exchange for rent, would take care of Steve and keep up the house. He decided Diana, Linda, and I could be put, temporarily, into a children's home. He would have put us all in the home but Steve was only two and still in diapers. The home wouldn't take children under five.

So, close to Christmas that year, we went to visit Augustana Lutheran Children's Home, in downtown Minneapolis, so we could see where we were going to be staying. It was an awesome building. It sat on a small hill with a wide sidewalk leading up to a large double door. A few feet above the door was a stained-glass window, about ten feet tall. It depicted Jesus sitting, surrounded by children looking lovingly up at him. I remember the words at the bottom of the window, *SUFFER THE LITTLE CHILDREN TO COME UNTO ME.*

When we entered the home there was a beautiful wooden staircase directly in front of us with a curved wooden railing leading up to the second floor. We were taken into the parlor to the left. It was a large, beautiful room with red velvet Queen Anne style furniture and a fireplace with a fire in it on the left wall. At the far end of the room was a huge Christmas tree that reached to the ceiling with hundreds of lights and ornaments! I had never seen such a beautiful tree. Everything was beautiful. Under the tree were hundreds of presents spreading half-way through the room. We were told they were all for the children in the home. Local Lutheran churches had taken the names of the children and bought them presents. Everything in this place was beautiful – like a gingerbread house.

When we went to sit down in the chairs, Sister Loraine smiled a patronizing smile and said, "Children are not allowed to sit on this furniture. It's for our adult visitors."

We took our places on the floor. When we left, I was anxious to get back. I imagined myself and bunches of happy, laughing kids sliding down the bannister in our pajamas and running into the living room to rip open all those presents. *This was going to be the best Christmas ever!*

In my excited anticipation, I missed the part where Sister Loraine told Dad not to bring us until after Christmas because the churches had already delivered the presents and it was too late to ask them to do a little last-minute shopping for the three of us. And Sister Loraine "wouldn't want us to be here with no presents to unwrap."

So, this was our first Christmas at home without Mother, heavy with sadness. The new family Christmas didn't start until Christmas-eve day when we'd get the cardboard fireplace down from the attic and set it up. Then dad would wait until just before the tree lots closed on Christmas Eve so he could buy a leftover tree for a dollar – sometimes even get it free. He'd also take a bunch of leftover branches. In the basement, he'd drill holes in the tree and insert branches until it was a perfectly good-looking tree. When we woke in the morning there would be the tree all decorated with a couple strings of regular lights and the string of ten bubble lights plus tinsel and a few glass ornaments. There was a present under the tree for each of us, but never anything we asked for or knew we wanted.

I learned many years later that Dad would go to the drugstore after we went to bed to buy us each a present. He said he had to wait until Christmas Eve to buy gifts because his dad sent money for Christmas but didn't want Dad wasting it on us, so he timed it to arrive at the last minute. Dad was supposed to buy something for himself. I think Grandpa didn't approve of Dad's choice of a wife and thought of Dad's children as a regrettable burden.

I still held out hope for the children's home. I thought all those kids with all those presents would surely let me play with them. I could hardly wait to see what they got!

Before we could enter the children's home, we needed blood tests. Dad took Diana, Linda, and me to a clinic. We didn't know what a blood draw was so when the nurse asked, "Who wants to be first?" Linda happily volunteered. She stood there smiling while the nurse stuck a big needle, with a huge bottle attached, into her arm.

"Oh, your little arm doesn't have enough blood. We'll just have to try the other arm now." Linda kept smiling as they poked holes all over her. I almost fainted at the sight. *I'm getting out of here before it's too late!*

I ran into the Ladies' Room, locked myself in a stall, and stood on the toilet so one of those wicked, smiley nurses couldn't grab me by the legs and drag me out.

Dad came into the bathroom (I was surprised. I thought he wasn't allowed in the ladies' room.) and yelled, "Janice, get out of there right now."

"No!"

He made Diana crawl under the door and open it. Then he dragged me out, kicking and fighting, back to the nurses, with me yelling, "No. No. No," all the way. They held me down and one of those wicked, smiley, nurses stuck the giant needle into my right arm and slowly sucked all the blood out.

When she finished, she taped a cotton ball over the big hole in my arm, saying, "Now that wasn't so bad was it?" She bent my arm and said, "Just hold it like this for a while."

As soon as she let go of my arm it went limp and just hung there.

"I can't. My arm is dead. You sucked all the blood out of my arm and killed it."

Dad, embarrassed that I "talked back" to the nurse that way, said, "Don't be stupid. Oh, just hold it up with your other hand."

My whole body was spent. I fought as hard as I could and still I was powerless. It took everything I had to walk back to the car. If my whole body felt this bad, my bloodless arm was surely dead.

I sulked all the way home, holding my arm to my chest and mad that I lost my best arm and nobody cared. *I want my mother.*

When we got home, Dad said, "Quit acting like a baby. Your arm's not dead."

"Yes, it is. And I can't keep holding it up forever. I need a sling."

So Diana made me a sling out of a dish towel. I was surprised when my blood filled my arm back up and by bedtime, I didn't need the sling any more.

| 12 |

No Great Christmas After All

Oblivious to the wonders that lay ahead, Diana, Linda, and I arrived at our new home, the Augustana Lutheran Children's Home, at the end of Christmas vacation in January 1950. Diana didn't want to go; I was hopeful, thinking of all those toys, and Linda was just happy to be with Diana and me. Sister Loraine greeted us at the door with a big smile, looking suspiciously like the witch in Hansel and Gretel, and invited us into her house made of candy. She was not pretty and looked older than Dad. Her hair was pulled back into a bun. She wore a white blouse, black skirt, and brown, lace-up shoes with a fat heel.

The home stood in the heart of downtown Minneapolis, surrounded by businesses, warehouses, and ancient, turn-of-the-century apartment buildings. It was built in 1923 to take care of children whose parents temporarily couldn't afford to keep them. That was us. Dad paid $7.00 per month for each of us. At the time, about twenty to twenty-five children were living there.

Standing in the front hall, we could see the parlor where the Christmas tree had been on the left. The big, beautiful staircase was in the center of the hallway. Between the parlor and the staircase was a door, I later found out, led to the back staircases (the children's staircases).

Directly opposite the parlor, on the right, was Sister Loraine's apartment. Between the staircase and Sister Loraine's apartment was a door, I later learned, leading to the dorm rooms where the boys slept.

After Dad left us there in the front hall that first day, Sister Loraine's smile vanished. *Hmm. I wonder if she has an oven.*

She said, "Take your belongings upstairs and Miss Ruth will show you where you sleep. After today, these stairs are for guests only. There is a staircase in the back that all you girls can use."

The second floor was for the girls and to the left of the wide center hall were the nursery, a dorm-style bedroom, a small "sick room," and the back stairwell. On the right were two private rooms for the girls' helpers, Miss Ruth, full time, and Miss Inez, part-time, and another dorm-style bedroom. I slept in the dorm room on the left, Diana slept in the dorm room on the right, and Linda slept in a crib in the nursery (even though she was five) with the twins, Dianne and Doreen (also five and in cribs).

I brought a little sock doll, I made in Brownies, from an old pair of Dad's black socks. I named her Anna.

When Sister Loraine saw her, she said, "We normally don't allow toys from home but I'll make an exception this time as long as you always leave it on your bed."

Soon I found out that all the Christmas toys the other kids received were gone, and the Home didn't have any toys. Everyone had to take their Christmas toys with them when they visited their parents after Christmas and weren't allowed to bring them back. I think they didn't have such a great Christmas either. They got a lot of new toys but had to leave them behind almost immediately. I thought that must be worse than not getting any toys.

Once, when the door to the boy's bedrooms was left open, I saw a little boy, George, sitting on a chair and crying. He was about Linda's age.

I asked, "What's wrong?"

"I'm being punished because my dad gave me a toy gun and let me bring here."

On hearing us, Sister Loraine came out of her room and said to George, "I told you there was no talking while you're being punished." And to me, "Janice, what are you doing here? Why aren't you in the playroom?"

"I wanted to ask you for a pencil and paper so I could draw."

"No, if I give you a pencil and paper everyone will want that and then there will be fights. We are all too busy to deal with that. Now go back to the playroom," she replied.

At bedtime, all the younger girls wanted my doll, especially Barbara, who slept in the bed next to me. "Please, please, can I have the doll to sleep with?" she begged relentlessly.

Finally, I gave her to Barbara and the next weekend she took her home and I never saw my little black sock doll again. I was disappointed but then, I DID give it to her and there was no reason why I should be the only one with a toy. I hope Barbara's mother didn't throw her away.

The entire back of the second floor was taken up by the girls' community bathroom with several sinks and toilets on one wall and three tubs in a row on the other wall.

Just like at home, Saturday night was bath night, except here we bathed by the timer – fifteen minutes. Miss Inez bathed Linda, Dianne, and Doreen, then the older girls took their baths three-at-a-time to the fifteen-minute timer. For the lucky ones that went home for the weekend, they were led immediately to the bathroom and bathed on Sunday; no chance to spread cooties.

Behind the bathroom was a screened-in porch which also ran the width of the building. This contained several huge cardboard boxes full of donated clothes from which we found our summer clothes for camp and I supposed, our winter clothes for school. The lucky kids that got their school wardrobe from these boxes had nice warm clothes. We did not.

Sister Loraine said, "Since the school year is half over and spring is almost here, there's no need to go to the trouble of fitting you three with a winter wardrobe, after all, you brought your winter clothes with you." Our winter wardrobe included coats, snow pants, hats, mittens, and rubber boots. No sweaters or warm socks.

All the girls at the children's home wore suspender style garter belts and long flesh-colored cotton stockings under their clothes. They had to wear them from the first day of school until school was out in June. But Diana, Linda, and I weren't outfitted with the belts and stockings. There were no spares and Sister Loraine didn't want to order any for us. Instead, we had to wear the snow pants we brought with us to school every day until it warmed up. I wanted the stockings! The other girls were jealous of us but I would have gladly traded their stockings (which they wore all day so their legs were always warm) for my snow pants which I kept on at school most days. My classroom wasn't very warm. Neither was the playroom.

Besides my winter outerwear, my school wardrobe consisted of the two summer dresses Dad bought me in August. They were identical dresses except one was pink striped and the other one was blue striped. I liked them because they had puffed sleeves, a ruffled yoke, and a circle skirt. Still, I envied the other girls their warm sweaters, corduroy jumpers, and long stockings.

The basement held the kitchen and dining room on the right and the boys' and the girls' playrooms on the left.

When we woke in the morning, the timer was set for fifteen minutes. We made our beds, dressed for school, and had to be down to the basement for breakfast before the timer went off.

After breakfast, Diana left for school. Before she would agree to be put in the home, Dad and Sister Loraine had agreed to let her take the bus (two transfers) to our old school, Lyndale, so she could graduate from sixth grade with her friends.

The rest of us put on our outer clothes in the hallway between the playroom and the dining room and set out for school. Miss Inez walked Linda, Dianne, and Doreen to school. They were in kindergarten. I walked alone. When we got home from school, we came in the back door and went directly to the basement where we took off our outer clothes and hung them on hooks in the hall – then into the playrooms to wait for dinner.

When Diana got home from school, she was paid ten cents a week to set the table for dinner and help clean up after dinner, so she never had to spend time in the playroom, which she would have hated. She saved her dimes and bought a necklace.

The girls' playroom had a half-wall, about three feet tall, that ran the length of the room, so we could always be seen from the hall. The door in the middle could only be opened from the outside. The girls' room had nothing – no books or dolls - not even pencils or crayons or paper, so we had nothing to fight over thus would need no supervision. An occasional staff member passing by the wall could suffice. The boys' playroom had a couple of trucks and a ball and no half-wall. I guess they didn't care if the boys killed each other. Since Diana was my only real friend at the Home, I usually sat quietly on the bench and tried to stay out of the little squabbles all around me. Judy and Sharon were older than me and best friends. They slept in the same room as Diana and didn't like her. They each had a younger sister, Barbara and Karen. They liked to make their sisters miserable and make fun of all the rest of the younger kids. For some reason, I was off limits and so was Linda. I don't remember but I must have said something to them. Plus, I was bigger than they were and wasn't above punching them.

At dinner time we stood behind our chairs to recite the blessing, "Come Lord Jesus, be our guest, and let this food for us be blessed. Amen."

Fifteen minutes to eat by the timer.

Sister Loraine would remind us, "No talking at the table and you can't drink your milk until your plate is clean. If anyone hasn't cleaned their plate before the bell goes off, you will go directly to bed after dinner."

After all the dishes were cleared away came a tablespoon of cod liver oil. After the first time, I said, "No thank you. I don't like it."

"You have to take it all winter. It's your dose of sunshine."

"Then I want to drink my milk after I have the cod liver oil."

"No."

Lastly, "God is great. God is good. We thank Him for our food. Amen."

Linda was a picky and slow eater and usually had to go directly to bed. At least she got to brush her teeth right away. The rest of us went to the playroom to wait for bedtime. I'm not sure which of us was being punished here, Linda having to go to bed early or me having to spend more time in the playroom and tasting cod liver oil until I could brush my teeth.

At seven o'clock the timer was set for the last time; fifteen minutes to put on our pajamas, brush our teeth, and say our prayers.

"Now I lay me down to sleep. I pray the Lord my soul to keep. If I should die before I wake, I pray the Lord my soul to take. And this I ask in Jesus' name, God bless Mother, Dad, Diana, Linda, and Steve. And please make Mother well so she can come home to us. Amen."

To the left of the home and across the alley was our private playground, surrounded by an eight-foot chain link fence. On Saturdays, school holidays, and sometimes after school, when the weather permitted, the girls were locked in there. The playground had a swing set and a sandbox, but I spent my time away from the other girls, hunting in the grass for four-leaf clovers. I needed some wishes granted.

Mostly I wished Mother would show up at the fence and say, "Janice, I've come to take you home." I was hoping that the more I wished for something, the better were the chances that my wish would be granted.

Sometimes the gardener/handyman for the children's home and the nursing home next door would bring his daughter, Doris, over and lock her in the yard with us. She looked about my age so I wondered why she would only approach one of the younger girls.

"Do you want to play house? Come with me." And she'd lead the chosen one into the bushes in the far corner of the playground to play house.

Once, I heard little Dianne crying and begging to leave. I got up and went into the bushes. "What's going on?"

"None of your business."

I took Dianne's hand. "You don't have to stay here if you don't want to."

Doris said, "You can't take her. I decide when she can leave."

"No you don't." "Come on, I'll push you on the swings," I said to Dianne as I led her out of the bushes.

The next time Doris was put in the yard, she asked Linda if she wanted to go in the bushes and play house. Of course Linda did so Doris started to lead her into the bushes.

I ran over there and said, "Linda, you can't go with her."

"I can too. I want to play house."

"She's not a nice person. She made Dianne cry, so you can't go into the bushes with her."

Doris yelled, "You aren't the boss here. I can do whatever I want. My dad runs this place and I'm going to tell him. You'll be in a lot of trouble."

"Okay, but Linda still can't play with you."

Linda really wanted to go so I said, "Why don't you come over there with me and help me look for four-leaf clovers? When you find one, you get to make a wish."

Reluctantly she went but didn't stay more than a couple of minutes. "This is boring. I want to play house," Linda whined.

"Well, you can't. Go play on the swing set," I said.

I was glad to be alone again with my clovers and wishes.

Doris never came back. She must have told her dad.

Diana, me (Janice), Linda

Doreen and Dianne

Sharon, Judy, Barbara

1950 Grade school pictures of a few of us residing at the children's home. Diana had saved them.

| 13 |

Billy

A few days after we entered the children's home, I started the second half of third grade at Madison Elementary. It was a five block walk. Maybe a week after I started school, I ran into a classmate, Billy, on my way to school. We instantly became friends, and he'd wait for me in front of his basement apartment every day so we could walk together. Billy liked to show off for me, and we laughed all the way to school. In school neither of us had any other friends, so we became good friends.

Billy couldn't read. Once a week our Reading Section included going around the room and reading a paragraph from our book. When Billy stood up to read, he'd pick up where the story left off and make up a wild and wonderful ending. I loved it and looked forward to his turn to read. So did everyone else – except the teacher. She'd tell him to stop.

"Billy, just read what's on the page or sit down."

Billy would "read" louder, all the while glancing at me to see if I still thought he was funny.

Then she'd yell, "Stop! You're not reading! Sit down!"

This only encouraged Billy, and he'd "read" even louder to drown out the teacher.

"If you don't stop now, I'll send you to the office."

That didn't faze Billy, so she'd snatch away his book. He'd smile at me and sit down. He liked making her mad. This went on for a few weeks until Billy noticed that the other students thought he was funny too and were egging him on. Then Billy started yelling back at the teacher when she took his book, telling her all the terrible things he was going to do to her.

"I'm going to stab you in the stomach and when you're lying on the floor dying, I'm going to cut your eyes out," etc.

I stopped laughing but Billy wasn't paying attention to me anymore. He was playing to the class and they didn't stop laughing. It was clear our teacher was afraid of Billy and he loved it.

After that outburst, the teacher asked me to stay after class. "I've seen how Billy listens to you. Can you make him stop?"

At first, I didn't know how to answer. I didn't want that role. Finally, I said, "He's my friend but I can't tell him what to do."

The next time Billy threatened her, she just ran out of the room and didn't come back. A sixth grader came in and told Billy to go to the principal's office, and she stayed to watch the class until the bell rang. I looked for Billy outside, but he didn't come out of the building. I never saw him again. Our teacher never told us what happened to Billy, and there was no one for me to ask. I could have gone down to his apartment and knocked on the door but by then I was a little afraid of him too. Those things he said to the teacher were scary. No one should talk to anyone like he talked to the teacher.

| 14 |

Summer Camp

Before school was out, and, in preparation for summer camp, Miss Inez took all us girls to a local beauty school to get our hair cut. One of Diana's jobs had been to braid everyone's hair before she left for school every morning. She hated the job and convinced Miss Inez we all needed short hair for the summer. I objected. I needed long braids so I could wear them wrapped in circles on the sides of my head like earmuffs. I refused to sit in the chair.

Miss Inez finally said, "We will just have your ends trimmed so that they are even. Not even an inch."

I sat down and the beautician cut my hair too short to braid. I cried and couldn't forgive the betrayal.

The day after school was out, the Home closed for the summer, and we all went to the Augustana Lutheran Children's Camp. Before we left, each of us went out on the back porch to get fitted for our summer wardrobe. We each got three outfits and a bathing suit. My favorite one was a three-piece blouse, skirt, and shorts. It was green striped piquet. The blouse tied in the front and left my stomach bare. The shorts were loose and hung almost to my knees and the skirt buttoned up the front. I could just button the top button and my shorts would show when I walked. I looked like a teenager. We laid out all our new summer clothes and our pillows on our mattresses. Then the staff came along and rolled them up, tied them with rope, and put our names on them. All but the very youngest were responsible for their bedroll, and we each carried it down to the waiting bus. We headed out of town to someplace south of Minneapolis, near a lake. With 10,000 lakes in Minnesota, I can't even guess as to where it was. I don't even know why I think it was south of town.

Bus rides were always a treat so we happily travelled down the road with high expectations about what lay ahead. About a quarter mile before reaching the Camp we passed by a small grocery store on the right and a little white church on the left, then over railroad tracks and down a hill past a huge pit to a big white farmhouse, or our wonderful camp.

As soon as I saw that pit littered with car parts, ice boxes, broken furniture, and any number of unidentifiable things, I poked Diana, "Look down there! This will be great!"

Diana didn't share my enthusiasm for trash but I knew I was going to have a great time at this camp.

The farmhouse sat facing a lake. We pulled up to the left side of the house and we all piled out, waiting for instructions.

"Girls, carry your bedrolls up the stairs to the screened-in porch. Pick out a cot and spread out your mattress. Kenny and Gary, carry your bedrolls out back to the cabin and do the same. The rest of you boys, follow me. I'll assign beds," barked Sister Loraine. "When you've finished making your beds, we'll have lunch ready."

The girls' dorm was a screened-in porch with canvas shades used in bad weather. When it rained, the staff rolled down the shades and had us pull our beds as far from the windows as possible. When it was cold, we covered up as best we could, rolling up in our blanket so we had more than one thickness of blanket.

The staff and the young boys slept in bedrooms on the first floor and about a hundred feet back behind the old farmhouse was the small one-room cabin where the older boys, Kenny and Gary, slept. About fifty feet behind the boys' cabin was a large, untended crop field of tall weeds.

On the left side of the farmhouse and in front of the trash pit stood two outhouses – one for the boys and one for the girls. Each one had three holes and a shower stall but no running water.

At the back of the house was a large rain barrel collecting rain water from the roof. If you lifted the wooden cover, you'd see it was full of floating, dead June bugs.

In front of the house was a small path through the overgrown lawn to the lake.

As soon as we were settled in, I ran to the pit. Although it was about ten feet deep, I was pretty sure I could slide down the side safely but couldn't see a way to get back out again. Nothing looked like it could be used as a make-shift ladder. If I called for help, someone would surely pull me out but they'd never let me keep whatever I went in there for.

When I was discovered sitting by the pit, Sister Loraine ordered, "Stay away from that trash pit. It's dangerous and you could fall in and die."

So, I took to sitting between the outhouses and the pit where I couldn't be seen from the house. After several days of daydreaming about what I could make from some of the trash, and with no possibility of ever having anything from the pit, I decided it was a waste of time, and my attention shifted to the rest of the camp.

On nice days we would walk single file down the path to the lake to play in the water. Since no one knew how to swim, including the staff, we were required to do twenty 'jump ups' before we could just play in the water.

We were instructed, "Go out into the water until the water is up to your armpits. Hold your nose and go down as far as you can then jump up while letting out your air, take a breath, and go back down. Do this twenty times, and then you can play in the water. If you ever get in water over your head, do this until someone comes to rescue you."

The water was freezing cold, so I thought it was a good way to warm up. Most of the other kids, especially the younger ones, were afraid to do it so just sat on the shore and played in the sand. I tried to swim but I just sank.

After a few visits to the lake, Barbara was covered with itchy sores and it was discovered that all along the path was poison ivy so Barbara couldn't go to the lake anymore. And she spent weeks covered in calamine lotion. The rest of us were shown what poison ivy looked like and told never to get off the path. If we got poison ivy, like Barbara, we could no longer go to the lake.

On Saturday morning, we'd each get a ten-cent allowance, provided our parents left money in a fund for us. Sister Loraine would bring out a box of white envelopes, each with one of our names on it. One at a time, she'd pull out an envelope, read the name, and look in the envelope.

"Audrey, here's your allowance. Karen, here's your allowance. Diana, Janice, and Linda, no allowance today. Barbara and Judy, here's your allowance," and so on.

Those of us who got an allowance (we all missed sometimes) would walk up the hill to the store and spend our dime on candy. We could get about a foot of candy dots on a strip of white paper for only a penny so a lot of kids bought at least one strip of that, even though they just tasted like a dot of sugar. And sometimes the paper stuck to the dot and you had to eat that too.

Everyone got a bath on Saturday night, whether we needed it or not. We went, one at a time, into the shower stall in the outhouse where Miss Inez had a pan of warm water. She used it to soap each of us down and shampoo our hair. Then she'd go to the rain barrel, push aside the bugs, fill the pan with the (freezing) water and dump it over our heads to rinse off. While I waited for the freezing rinse-off, I thought about grabbing my towel and running off. But I couldn't. My pajamas were sitting there and I couldn't get them on before Miss Inez would be back.

Every Sunday we'd put on our best clothes and walk up the hill to Sunday school. The other kids (the ones that lived there all the time) didn't like us very much and avoided talking to us. I kept hearing their parents reminding them they had to be nice to us. It puzzled me but I didn't much care. They were all mean and stupid.

The rest of our time was spent outdoors unless it was raining. "You need to be out in the sunshine. Otherwise, we'll have to give you cod liver oil." *Sunshine is good.*

Once, a new boy named Jerry was brought to the Camp by his dad. I was so excited. He was my age and had flaming red, curly hair. I loved boys with red hair and hoped I finally had someone to play with.

I sang, "Here comes Jerry Carrot Top ….," every time I saw him, hoping he'd chase me or at least tell me I was stupid. But he cried instead. I thought he'd get over it but he didn't and his father came and got him.

| 15 |

The Nutgoodie

It was beginning to look like the Camp was not much better than the Home when it came to being "bored," so I took to crawling around in the tall weeds behind the farmhouse, hoping to come across a bunny or some other animal in distress – or maybe even some dwarves or fairies living there. It was disappointing that I couldn't find even a cricket or frog until one day I finally found something! It was an old iron cot with a set of bedsprings! I felt like it had risen out of the trash dump and was just waiting for me to find it. I laid on the bare bedsprings to think, watching the clouds change shape and looking for inspiration. The grass was so tall no one could see me, so I did this for several days until I finally had an idea. I could produce the play, *The Princess and the Pea*. The cot was perfect for this.

"Diana, I have a great idea. I found an old cot out in that field. We can use it to put on a play, *The Princess and the Pea*. What do you think? We can make the costumes out of crepe paper. I saw that the store sells crepe paper for five cents a package."

Being just as bored as I was, she agreed to help. We told everyone that whoever would spend half their ten-cent allowance on crepe paper could be in the play. It took at least three weeks to get enough crepe paper for all the costumes. Linda was the princess, and Barbara was the prince because none of the boys wanted to be in the play, much less give up any of their money. Diana and I made the costumes as soon as the crepe paper became available. On the day of the play, Diana and I went out into the tall grass to drag the iron cot into the backyard under the big tree. We had kept the cot a secret for fear it would be taken to the dump once it was discovered. We put layers of blankets from our beds on the springs, and the staff put out folding chairs for the audience. Everyone attended. The older boys from the cabin wouldn't sit on the chairs but instead climbed the tree behind the "stage." I objected but the staff didn't care and refused to make them get out of the tree so the play went on.

We never had a dress rehearsal because we didn't want to ruin the costumes. Besides, no one wanted to practice their lines. When Barbara realized she had to take all her clothes off except her underwear in order to wear the paper costume, she didn't want to be in the play. No one knew where they were supposed to stand and of course no one knew their lines. Everything was going wrong! I finally got Barbara into her costume, placed everyone where they were supposed to stand, and started whispering everyone's lines to them.

After Barbara said, "Fair princess, here is your bed. Sleep well," she bowed to the princess.

Her paper pants split wide open and at that same moment, the boys in the tree shot her in the behind with spitballs! She jumped up with her hands over the split and ran screaming into the house. Everyone, including the staff, laughed and laughed. I didn't see anything funny about ruining my play and was so angry. I don't remember anything more about the play except it was over.

Everyone clapped and Sister Loraine got up and thanked us all for the "wonderful" play.

Turning to me, she said, "Janice, we all enjoyed your play, *The Princess and the Pea*. Here is something to reward you for all your hard work."

And she presented me with a Nut Goodie candy bar. I was confused, embarrassed, and somehow proud. Out of all my good ideas, this was the biggest disaster and, yet, it was the only one I ever received an award for. I was confused about why I would be rewarded for this disaster, but, still, I saved my Nut Goodie like a baseball trophy, hidden in my underwear drawer so it wouldn't be stolen and eaten.

| 16 |

The Revival

Miss Inez loved all of her charges. Even more, Miss Inez loved God. So when she heard there was an evangelical revival tent coming to an area near the Camp, she decided to take any of us girls that wanted to go, for an overnight campout near the revival. We all wanted to go! We didn't know what a revival was, but we all wanted to go camping!

She arranged for a local farmer to take us and all our camping equipment on his flatbed truck to a field near the revival and pick us up in the morning. We set up our tents and were going to build a fire and roast marshmallows and drink hot chocolate when we got back from the revival. What an adventure!

As the sun was setting, we went with Miss Inez in the lead. The big tent was already filling up with people and we sat near the back. When everyone was seated, the preacher came out and began yelling about salvation and the devil!

"Turn from your wicked ways! Repent and you shall be saved!"

It was an exciting spectacle with people jumping up and down and yelling, "Amen!" and "Save me Jesus!" and "Help me Lord!"

The preacher begged everyone to come to the front who were ready to have their sins washed away and be born again. Many ran to the stage and laid down on the floor in the sawdust.

"Save me Jesus! I'm a sinner!"

And it began to pour outside the tent with thunder and lightning and heavy winds! What a show! We were awestruck! After all, we were Lutherans and didn't know what to think of this. Yelling in church was a no-no. Running up and throwing yourself on the floor was too. But with the big show going on outside the tent as well as the one within, God must have loved the spectacle too.

Miss Inez encouraged us to go up front to be saved, but none of us did. Later Diana said she wanted to be saved and born again but was afraid that she would sin after she was saved and then she'd go to hell. She decided to wait until she was going to die and then she'd get saved.

Shortly before the show was over, it stopped raining. God probably decided the show was over so we walked back to our campsite. Everything was wet, even inside the tents. There was nothing dry to start a fire with so we couldn't have our marshmallow roast and hot chocolate. We just went to bed, wet blankets and all. Then the rain came back and our tents started leaking again. The rain hit on the tent and with every drop a fine mist fell on us. I rolled up my clothes and used them as a pillow to keep my head up off the ground so I wouldn't accidentally drown in my sleep. Linda cried and went to sleep in Miss Inez's lap. When morning finally came, we didn't have breakfast because we still couldn't make a fire. We were so cold. The farmer eventually came to get us. When we got back home, dry clothes and warm blankets never felt so good. Audrey, the shy, sickly girl, got pneumonia and went to the hospital. She never came back.

| 17 |

Home Again

Summer vacation was over. We climbed on the bus with our bedrolls stowed below us and took our sad ride back to the Home. Diana, Linda, and I didn't stay long though. We were sent back home before school started.

Diana turned twelve in June, and the Home wouldn't let anyone over twelve live there. They had made an exception for Diana so we could stay for the entire summer at the Camp.

Dad hired Miss Ruth, one of the staff at the Home. None of us liked her, but at least we were going home. At home, all the rules from the Home came with Miss Ruth. The timer in the kitchen gave us fifteen minutes to get dressed and down to the kitchen in the morning. Then the timer gave us fifteen minutes to eat breakfast, fifteen minutes to get our stuff together and outerwear on and out the door to school. One can only imagine what life was like when we were in school and little Steve was alone with her all day.

I caught Miss Ruth spanking Steve with a hairbrush because he wet his diaper. I told Dad but he did nothing. Us girls (mostly me) were constantly being punished by Miss Ruth, for who knows what. Punishment involved sitting on a chair in the living room for hours without anything to do and "No talking!" Talking wasn't a problem unless more than one of were being punished at the same time – which happened more often than you'd expect. We'd have to get permission to go to the bathroom. Sometimes I could sneak a pencil and paper in with me when being punished. When I had to go to the bathroom, I hid the pencil in my sock. Then, on one occasion, on the way upstairs I stepped on the pencil and broke the lead off in my foot. I collapsed on the stairs and screamed like Hell. I was surprised to find that Miss Ruth was more upset than I was. Instead of earning another hour in the chair, she tried to get the lead out and kept begging me not to tell Dad. I did anyway. After many more incidents, Dad finally asked Miss Ruth to leave. She wouldn't go, so Dad had to call her father to come and get her. I can still see the pencil lead in my foot.

The Rangers lived next door to us. Mr. Ranger owned the take-out chow mein store on the other side of the block. Mrs. Ranger had had a "nervous breakdown" and was in the same mental hospital as Mother.

The kids said, "Mom wasn't crazy though. She was suffering from depression and wanted to commit suicide."

Somehow, they thought that made her better than our mother. And lucky for us, Mrs. Ranger came home and their housekeeper, Rene, was available.

| 18 |

The Golden Rule

I was back at Lyndale Grade School for fourth grade. Painted in bold letters and running about half-way down the hall was, *THE GOLDEN RULE – DO UNTO OTHERS AS YOU WOULD HAVE THEM DO UNTO YOU.* It started at the top of the entrance stairs and ran past the principal's office and past the nurse's office. On my first day of school I read it and was so impressed by it – I never knew there was a Golden Rule. It was in blue letters on a fancy yellow strip with blue Greek scroll work on the top and bottom, just about at fourth grade eye level.

I must have started fourth grade a few days late because everyone was in their seats when I was brought into the classroom.

Right away the teacher asked me if I knew the difference between a fruit and a vegetable. I didn't. She grabbed me by the arm and marched me right back to the principal's office and said, "Janice doesn't belong in my class! She doesn't even know basic third grade stuff, and I don't have the time to teach her! Put her back in third grade where she belongs."

"Just give her a chance to catch up. Maybe one of the other students can work with her." said Miss Putnam, the blue haired principal.

She grudgingly took me back to class. At recess I went with the teacher to the third-grade room where she complained to the third grade teacher about me, so I was given a third-grade textbook.

"Take this home and learn about fruits and vegetables. I'll test you next Monday. If you pass, you can stay in my class."

I guess my fourth-grade teacher didn't come to her classroom the same way I did because I could tell she never read the wall.

"Diana, you need to help me learn the difference between a fruit and a venchtable before next Monday or I'll have to go back to 3rd grade!"

"Okay, but first, you need to learn how to say vegetable."

We sat at the dining room table with a pencil and paper.

"Here, I'll write it down and you sound out the word."

"ven—"

"No, do you see an 'N'?"

"I didn't say 'N'."

"Yes you did – start again."

| 19 |

Who's Your Mama?

As I made new friends at Lyndale Grade School, I began to notice that I was treated differently by some of my new friends' mothers. Many felt compelled to mother me as soon as they found out my mother was gone. I didn't understand. I still have a mother, and she'll be back any day now. Then when she didn't come back and didn't come back, I began to resent these almost-strangers thinking Mother could easily be replaced by them. I knew they didn't want to be my mother. They hardly knew me. For sure they didn't love me.

"Janice, 'Joannie' tells me your mother is in the hospital. That's so sad. Just remember, if you need someone to talk to, you can always come to me."

Or say things like, "I know your mother would want you to do/say ……." - as if they even knew my mother.

I finally came to the conclusion that what they wanted was to show their own daughters how lucky they were to have their mothers and how much smarter and better mannered they were than me because of it.

"You would be so pretty if you stood up straight/combed your hair/said 'thank you' more/cleaned your nails/polished your shoes," etc. and etc.

"You and 'Joannie' can do your homework together here." This ploy was more to (hopefully) find out that their child was much smarter than me. But usually 'Joannie' needed my help with her homework.

And then there were the ones who wanted to pity me and hoped to make me cry. "You poor thing! How hard it must be!"

I met a new girl, Janet, at school and she invited me to her house one day. She said her father was a Presbyterian minister. Almost immediately, her mother said she was sorry to hear about my mother.

Then she said, "You would really be a pretty girl if you would just stand up straight. Your round, sagging shoulders ruin your looks." I was embarrassed.

Sometimes teachers wanted to be my mother too. Their motivation seemed more of a way to control me in the classroom. I couldn't avoid the teachers who aspired to take my mother's place, but I could walk away from any new friend and her mother, which I did.

There were only two women who loved me the way I imagined a mother would, and I loved them back, Anna, our first permanent housekeeper and Dorothy's mother. Dorothy and I met in Brownies in third grade and were 'best friends forever.' Dorothy was the only daughter of immigrant parents from Sweden. Her parents cleaned offices for a living - her mother worked days and her father worked nights - so she came home every day to an empty house.

Sometimes I'd stop at Dorothy's (there was always a snack left out), and then we'd go on to my house where we usually had some project in the works.

At school and at our Brownie, then Girl Scout meetings, we were always looking for ways to push the envelope and make things more 'interesting.' They were almost always my ideas, but Dorothy willingly took 50% of the blame.

Once, at a Girl Scout weekend campout, I threw our leader Mrs. Johnson's young daughter's doll in the latrine. Cindy was a spoiled brat, probably about four. Mrs. Johnson brought her to all the meetings, and everyone had to defer to whatever Cindy demanded in order to avoid a temper tantrum. I was tired of it, so when I went to the out-house and found her doll sitting there, I dropped it in. When it was finally found, they blamed me.

"I didn't do it! Why do I always get blamed for everything?"

"Because it's always you."

I had to clean the latrine for the rest of the weekend. I think they only had to look at our faces to know the truth. Dorothy helped me clean, and we thought it was worth it.

Troup 548

Whenever we got in trouble for misbehaving, we'd run to Dorothy's mother with our version of events. She'd get so mad at everyone (except us) for the way we were treated.

She'd get on the phone, "Quit picking on my girls! You think just because I work and Janice's mother is in the hospital you can blame everything on them! Shame, shame on you!" She refused to even listen to their excuses. I love her still for those calls.

| 20 |

Rene

Our new housekeeper was Rene. Rene was a German lady from the predominantly German town of Waseca, Minnesota.

Rene had a teenage son, Wally that stayed back in Waseca with someone in Rene's family. Rene said Wally's father was struck by lightning – twice! The second time he didn't survive. Wally had a different last name than Rene, and she never referred to Wally's father as her husband.

Diana instantly fell in love with her. When Diana came home from school on Rene's first day, the house was spotless, something we had not seen since Mother was well. Needless to say, I didn't notice, but Diana remembers with fondness to this day.

We were so fortunate to have found her. She worked non-stop and all for $25.00 per week. Monday was for laundry, Tuesday for ironing, Wednesday for baking, Thursday for cleaning, and I can't remember Friday. Saturday and Sunday were her days off but she usually worked anyway. She made us breakfast, lunch, and dinner every day. Every dinner was meat, potatoes, and a vegetable. Dessert was either cake, pie, cookies or canned fruit.

Rene got the empty flour sacks from the grocery store and made pillow cases which she embroidered and edged with crocheted lace in her spare time. Dad said he didn't like them because the embroidery was scratchy on his face. I thought they were great. She read "True Crime" magazines.

We got the first TV in the neighborhood, a six-inch Motorola with a magnifying glass hung in front. Rene loved watching wrestling, and we all tried to sit next to her. She'd yell at Gorgeous George, Verne Gagne, and Killer Kowalski and grab our legs, kick us and put us in a choke hold. We loved the horse play - something in short supply in our lives.

Rene decided girls should have curls, so, as needed, she'd give us permanents. One time she left my permanent in too long, and I ended up with a huge head of kinky, wooly hair. I loved it! I could brush it straight up and pin it up with bobby-pins so all the wool was on top of my head. It was the latest style – the Upsweet, or as I was soon informed, "It's Upsweep not Upsweet, and you're not old enough to wear your hair that way. It's a grown-up hair style."

Every Saturday morning I walked through the alley, looking in the neighbors' trash cans for useful stuff. One cold January, I found a gunny sack with something in it. When I opened it, I found a frozen puppy! She had little blond ears. I think she was a golden retriever. It was bitterly cold outside, and the puppy was frozen as solid as a block of ice. I imagined there must have been some terrible accident that had allowed her to freeze like this. It was twenty degrees below zero, and she was such a small puppy. Maybe she would still be alive if she was thawed out; after all, babies come alive after they are born when they are made to cry.

"Trash Can, I'll call you Trash Can," I whispered to her.

I had been hearing about the new science of freezing and bringing back to life things like frogs. Was it possible? Would God be mad? Scientists thought that someday they would figure out how to freeze and revive even a whole person. So, I brought Trash Can home. I made a bed of rags in a box and put her in front of the radiator in the kitchen.

When Rene saw the puppy she said, "Get that dead thing out of my kitchen!"

"No. I'm thawing her out and then I'll have a puppy."

"I'm going to tell your dad when he gets home." She always said that.

I relented and took Trash Can down to the basement and placed her by the furnace. It wasn't as warm down there but it would have to do. When Dad came home, she told him anyway.

He said, "That dog is dead and will stink up the whole basement once it thaws out."

He took her back to the alley and chucked her in a trash can. *How would HE know?* What if Trash Can thawed out at the dump and then died a slow and horrible death, alone and cold and hungry? I tried not to think about that.

I would never find out if my puppy could have lived, but for a long time afterward I listened and read with interest about the advancements of cryogenics and wondered if Trash Can would have made history.

Back when we moved home from the children's home, my award (a Nutgoodie candy bar) came with me, still hidden in my underwear. When Rene found it, she said I needed to throw it out.

"No. I'm saving it."

"I'm going to tell your dad." She told Dad.

He said, "Throw that old candy bar out before it attracts mice, ants, or roaches."

That wasn't happening so I decided it was time to eat my award. Funny thing though – when I finally unwrapped it, someone had already taken a giant bite out of it. I wonder if Sister Loraine did that. I don't know - maybe I did.

| 21 |

Babe

When Dad's number came up for the draft, Mother said, "He was 4F because he was too skinny." Dad was 5'9" and weighed 123 pounds. I think the real reason was because he was married with two children.

Babe said, "I decided to join the WACs because Les couldn't go."

Her first years as a WAC in Fort Wayne, Indiana, she went door-to-door trying to convince other women to join the WACs. After that, she became a decoder stationed in Pearl Harbor, and was there on December 7th.

Babe came to visit us after the war was over and she was on leave. She brought her friend. Her friend was big and loud and rude. When they came down for breakfast that first morning, Babe's friend looked at the table and said to Rene, "I don't drink prune juice for breakfast. Get me a glass of orange juice. And I don't eat cream of wheat either. Fix me bacon and eggs and biscuits."

We (me, Diana, Linda, and Steve) were sitting at attention, waiting for Rene's response. Ooo she was mad! I'd never seen Rene mad before.

"If you don't like what you're served, you're free to eat elsewhere."

We were proud of her, and it was hard not to smile. We couldn't figure out why Babe would have a friend like that.

They left that day (her friend in a huff) and headed up to Grandpa Druley's, in Oregon, for a visit. We heard that didn't go well either. Grandpa's wife Hautye (pronounced haughty) threw them out and said she and Grandpa were disowning Babe and she was no longer welcome in their home.

"They're disgusting and I won't allow such filth in my home." Hautye said.

I didn't know what they had done that would be so bad that Grandpa would disown his daughter, Babe. I could understand asking her friend to leave, but what had Babe done?

| 22 |

The Family Car

In 1951, Dad decided we needed a car big enough for the whole family. With limited funds, he bought a 1938 Cadillac hearse.

Hearse in the driveway

"It has a great engine and very low mileage," Dad said.

It was beautiful with a shiny black exterior, red velvet floors, walls, and ceiling, plus red velvet curtains on the windows. In the back there was a soft, baby blue, velvet, fold-up seat for one and there was even a back door. There was a sound-proof sliding window between the front seat and the back. I loved our car just the way it was. I thought I could live in there.

"Can I sleep in here tonight?"

"No."

Dad had other plans for our beautiful new car. First, he tried to remove the rollers on the floor but it was going to be an enormous job, so he glued linoleum over the whole velvet floor. Then he bought and bolted to the floor two streetcar seats. He threw away the velvet curtains, much to my objection.

When he finished, we went on our first ever vacation to visit Aunt Helen in International Falls. Diana got to ride in the front seat and kept the sound-proof window closed which bummed me out. I had to listen to Linda and Steve fight all the way to International Falls. When we stopped to eat the lunch Rene had packed, Linda and Steve had eaten the whole pan of chocolate chip bars.

Years later, when I decided to get all my relatives to write limericks to put in a limerick book, Diana and I wrote this limerick about the family car:

> My father for us bought a hearse
> To Diana, at 13, 'twas a curse
> She hid, ducking down
> As we drove about town
> 'Cause her friends thought it was even worse
>
> We siblings thought it was the best
> On the blue velvet seat we would rest
> I'd wave out the door
> Yell, "Diana's on the floor!"
> If she could she would strangle this pest
>
> Once we traveled to Aunt Helen Eeles'
> On those bus seats we ate all our meals
> We read plates on cars
> Fought o'er chocolate chip bars
> And with trading cards worked our big deals

| 23 |

Mother's Teeth

While her children were navigating their new definition of life, so was Mother. One of her many traumas was her teeth.

Mother lamented, "I had such beautiful teeth. They were perfectly straight, and I never had even one cavity. I don't know why they had to be pulled."

She lost her upper teeth while in Rochester State Hospital. Dental students were allowed to "practice" on mental patients in the state hospitals as long as they had the guardian's permission. One day they brought her to a dental office set up in the hospital where dental students from the local college took turns drilling on her teeth. First one student would drill a tooth to a point, then the next student would step in and drill another tooth to a point until all fourteen of her upper teeth were drilled to points.

Mother said, "When they were finished with me, I looked like a wolf!"

Then several times more she was taken to the makeshift dental office and they took turns pulling all her (now) pointed teeth. When all her upper teeth were gone, they made her false teeth.

Mother had lost all her rights as a human because she was 'put' in the hospital and didn't go voluntarily. She couldn't vote, and all her mail was censored. If she wrote anyone to complain about the conditions at the hospital, her letter was destroyed.

Mother said, "They told me my teeth needed to be removed to prevent me from biting anyone. Why would I bite someone? I'm not a child."

She was violated, but no one cared so she quit talking about it.

| 24 |

"Please Release Me, Let Me Go"

Please Release Me, Let Me Go, the Johnny Ray song from the 50's, should have been Mother's song.

Mother was discharged fourteen times during her fifteen-year stay in State Hospitals. Twelve of those times were during her ten year stay at St. Peter State Hospital. Dr. Grimes would tell Dad that Mother was no longer mentally ill and could come home. Legally, she couldn't just be released because she was 'cured.' Once in a mental hospital, patients lost their autonomy and only their legal guardians could remove them from the hospital. For a woman, that person was almost always her husband. I don't know if the same laws applied to men (that their wives were their guardians), but somehow, I doubt it.

Whenever we went to pick Mother up in Rochester, we waited outside. Whenever we came to St. Peter to bring Mother home after she was released, we (us kids) were left in the waiting room while Dad went to talk to the only licensed psychiatrist at the hospital. At Rochester, that was Dr. Peterson, and at St. Peter, that was Dr. Grimes. The waiting room at St. Peter was a large open area with only a few chairs along the walls. Most of the chairs were occupied by residents waiting for someone to pick them up or just waiting (for life to be over,

I guess). At one end was a glass case with items made by the residents and for sale. Everyone in the room looked so sad and some seemed to be asleep with their eyes open. Some wanted to touch us and talk to us, so we smiled and responded. They were Mother's friends.

"You must be Millie's children!"

"You're all so beautiful."

"Just look at that curly hair."

"You look so much like my daughter. I haven't seen her in such a long time."

"I'm a friend of your mother's."

"She is such a lovely person."

"I'm going to miss her."

Once, Mother took us back to see her bedroom. When we noticed that there were no dressers or closets, she explained that everyone kept all their belongings in a box under their bed.

"If you don't want your things stolen, you keep them in your purse and carry them with you at all times."

Mother took her meager belongings and when Dad came back from the doctor's office, we all piled back in the car. Their fighting would begin before we even got out of the parking lot.

"You son-of-a-bitch. You didn't send me cigarette money for more than a month. I couldn't buy cigarettes and had to bum them or smoke the butts in the ash trays."

I remember one time especially: "Do you even care about what happened to me three months ago? Some Goddamn crazy bitch decided I stole her nose and she tried to rip my nose off. Of course I fought back and that nasty nurses' aide, the one that hates me, put me in the straight jacket and set me up for shock treatments. Even the aides can order shock treatments in this hell-hole. And you, you ass hole! You said, 'Fine. Go ahead with the shock treatments.'

Bedrooms in St. Peter

As soon as I get home, I'm divorcing your sorry ass."

"Don't swear in front of the kids."

We kids were so excited to have her back. Mother always had the radio on playing the latest music. She had a good voice and would sing along. Diana and I were anxious to talk to her about events in our lives and get her feedback; we had waited so long. Mother would spend most of the day smoking and listening to the radio or talking on the phone with her mother and sisters.

Dad would come home from work and dinner was unprepared. The laundry was not done. The house was a mess with dirty dishes on the table and the beds unmade. Steve was largely ignored. Then the fighting started again.

"What are you doing all day?" Did you even feed Steve?"

She would yell back, "I'm so sick of you. Just give me a divorce and we'll all be fine."

"You're not taking these kids anywhere. You're not a fit mother."

If only someone would have said Mother needed our help, we would have gladly done anything to keep her home. The sad truth was, Dad didn't want her home, so Mother never stayed long. Dad would take her back to the hospital as soon as he could. I believe he goaded her into fighting so he could haul her back to the hospital claiming she had another breakdown.

When she would get back to the hospital, she'd be angry. The doctors tried out all the newest mood-altering drugs to calm her down, putting her into a semi-catatonic state. Then, when she was quiet, they'd try to send her back home. Fourteen times, all the same. And still we prayed for God to make her well.

| 25 |

Bambi's Child

In the summer of 1951, I had the chance to go to welfare camp. It was great! A bus came right to our doors and picked each of us campers up. Then we rode out to an old Boy Scout camp in the country. We didn't even need to bring our own beds. The entrance to the camp was a long driveway lined with tall poplars that made wonderful rustling sounds in the wind - something I enjoyed laying on the lawn and listening to when I ran out of other things to do. At the end of the drive was a large open lawn lined on either side with woods and sloping to a big beach on a small lake or river. Looking toward the lake, all the camp buildings were lined up on the left. First was the mess hall, then the craft building, the nurse's cabin, and the lodge. Halfway to the lake was the bunk house. All the buildings were made with logs, just like in a Gene Autry movie. And in the center of the lawn was a playground with swings, slides, monkey bars, and a sand box. I knew I was going to have a wonderful time! This was SO much better than the children's home camp!

The first thing we did was get settled in the bunk house. The first floor was for the counselors and staff. The second floor was for us campers. It was a big open room filled with bunk beds. I grabbed an upper bunk.

The camp was run by the Minnesota state welfare system, and I got to go to this camp because I was a welfare child. My family went on welfare after we came home from the children's home. With Mother in the hospital and four children and a live-in housekeeper, Dad couldn't keep up with the bills, so he applied for welfare assistance. And that's how I got to go to camp!

At camp we all got up and dressed and made our beds (I was rethinking the wisdom of having a top bunk), and then we'd all march in a row to the mess hall for breakfast – no prayers and plenty of talking. The rest of the day was filled with games and swimming and free time to play on the playground. Some nights we'd have a campfire and hear stories and roast marshmallows. I was having a great time!

When it rained, we'd go to the lodge and have a big fire in the fireplace and play board games or read books from the small library. That's where I found *Bambi's Children.* I took it back to the bunk house to read. It was the saddest book I'd ever read! Right at the beginning, Bambi's wife hid her twins in a safe place and told them not to move. She went out to forage for food and was killed by hunters! Not knowing what happened to their mother, the fawns stayed hidden for a very long time until they finally were so hungry they had to find something to eat. Out in the open, they had one harrowing adventure after another while trying to find their mother.

I'd sit on my bunk so no one could see me crying while I read, but sometimes it was so sad I'd have to sob out loud.

One of the campers told the counselors, "Janice is sitting on her bed crying all the time."

"What's wrong?" they asked me.

"Nothing, I'm not crying. I have a cold."

I was taken to the nurse. She asked if I was homesick and offered to have the bus take me home or have my dad come and get me.

"I'm fine. I don't want to go home."

I didn't tell them about *Bambi's Children* because I was sure they would take the book away and then I'd never know what happened to them. I HAD to know. Finally, the nurse and the counselors decided I should sleep with the nurse in her cabin. My bed was the one reserved for anyone who got sick at camp – fortunately no one was sick at that time. Everything in the room was white and I had a curtain I could pull all around the bed if I wanted.

Every time the nurse needed to go somewhere, she'd say, "I need to go (wherever) but I won't go if you need me to stay with you. I won't be gone long."

"I'll be okay."

Secretly I was glad to see her go so I could get back to my book. As soon as the door closed, I'd pull my book out from its hiding place under my pillow. By the time the nurse returned, I'd be sitting there with swollen, red eyes. And she'd be upset.

"I thought you said you'd be fine. What's the matter? Please tell me so I can help you."

"Nothing's wrong. I just have sinus problems."

FINALLY I was able to finish the book. Bambi's children got through all their scary adventures and grew up and had their own children and everyone was very happy.

I told the nurse I was well and wanted to go back to the bunk house. On my way, I returned the book to the lodge.

When camp was over, we were told the next round of camping was not full so we could stay if we wanted to. I wanted to, but they wouldn't let me stay. They thought I needed to go home.

| 26 |

Show and Tell

Mother's sewing machine sat forlorn and forgotten in the corner of the dining room. That is, until Diana, in seventh grade, was required to take sewing and cooking. She began enthusiastically practicing on Mother's machine. I watched with interest, remembering Mother at her sewing machine. So, that summer, between fourth and fifth grade, I was rummaging through the attic looking for something to do and found a rag doll pattern! I asked Diana to show me how to use the sewing machine and how to read the pattern. She was happy to. I got my fabric from the rag barrel in the basement – an old white sheet. I charged some RIT dye at the grocery store and dyed the sheet Peach (nobody's skin is really pink). Using the sewing machine was hard and frustrating. The thread was always getting knotted up, and, once I sewed right through my left index fingernail! I'd yell and swear at the machine and hit it.

"If you don't quit hitting the sewing machine and swearing at it, you can't use it!" Diana would yell.

I'd get out the little screwdriver that came with the machine and take every screw I could find out. By then I was calmed down, and I'd start to worry about getting it back together. By the time I had it put together again, I was ready to give it another try.

It took a long time to sew the doll and I stuffed her with more rags from the rag barrel. This made her so heavy that her head wouldn't stay up, and I was afraid the material would rip so I took her apart and put wooden dowels in her head/torso and her legs. I got yarn and sewed on her hair. I took her to Susan's mother and asked her to teach me to embroider her face. I named her Anna. When I had her finished, I went back to the rag barrel to find material to make her clothes. The pattern had a whole wardrobe, but I could only find enough material for a blouse, skirt, panties, and shoes. I used my brother's baby socks. This all took up the rest of my summer.

I could hardly wait for school to start so I could take my doll for Show-and-Tell. When the day finally arrived, I put Anna in a paper bag and brought her to school. I didn't want anyone to see her until The Great Unveiling.

When my turn finally came, I pulled her out of the bag and said, "I made her myself!"

The teacher said I was lying – I didn't really make her – and until I told the truth about where I got the doll, I needed to put her back in the bag and take her home. So I did.

If Mother had been home, she would have called my teacher and told her to apologize to me – no, she would have marched me back to school and gotten right in the teacher's face and demanded an apology! I don't remember my fifth-grade teacher's name, but I'll always remember that I never liked her.

| 27 |

Show and Tell II

During the spring of fifth grade I had a new inspiration! While on my regular rounds through the alley trash cans, I found ANOTHER set of bedsprings propped against a trash can (similar to the ones from children's camp, except no bedframe). I dragged the bedsprings home. I was busy setting free each spring when Dad got home from work. "Put that back where you found it! This yard isn't the dump!" he yelled. I had managed to remove eight or ten springs by then, so I hid them before returning the carcass to its place by the neighbor's trash can.

Pat and Jerry at Garden Grocery saved their fruit crates for me, and I'd go by whenever I had a new "project" and pick them up. I'd carefully pull all the straight nails and save them for any future projects.

Dorothy, my ever-willing partner in crime, and I nailed two springs each to four peach crate boards, cut to the general length of our feet. We tied the boards to our shoes and spent a lot of time trying to jump up and down without the springs shooting out one side or another and breaking the boards or twisting an ankle. Finally, we tied each pair of springs together and nailed them on a bottom board. That helped a lot.

Just jumping up and down got boring fast and didn't seem flashy enough for Show-and-Tell yet.

After hunting for inspiration, we found a couple of bubble pipes in Steve's toy box. Now we could jump up and down singing I'm *Forever Blowing Bubbles* while blowing bubbles out of the pipes.

Everyone loved our Show and Tell even though I was suddenly struck with shyness and didn't sing – only laughed, jumped, and blew bubbles.

The teacher sent Dorothy alone to the other classroom to perform. "Dorothy, that was so entertaining! Why don't you go and show it to the other fifth grade class? Janice, you don't need to go."

Once again, I keenly knew this was all about my teacher not liking me. And this would have been the last straw for Mother! She would have demanded I be moved to another fifth-grade classroom.

| 28 |

Body Image

Around age eleven or twelve, Dorothy started to have a body image crisis. She developed boobs and started to have to wear a bra. They were pretty big all of a sudden. All the boys were teasing her and the girls were jealous. Her hips got bigger too, or maybe just more shapely. I was glad it wasn't me. Dorothy thought her calves were too fat also. We decided we would exercise our legs in order to make hers thinner.

Every Saturday we'd ride 10 or more miles, but it didn't work. Her calves kept growing but mine didn't. I wanted big calves. Dorothy's mom scraped together the money to let Dorothy go to a weight-loss clinic. It sounded like fun, but of course my family couldn't afford it. I didn't even need to ask.

I went with her sometimes to watch her exercise. At the clinic, Dorothy put a belt around her hips, and it vibrated really fast to wear off the fat. What a great idea! So much easier than pedaling up and down hills all day – but it didn't work either.

We went back to riding bikes on Saturday but got bored with that. It was a waste of time we decided. Dorothy sadly had to live with the fact that she was becoming an adult. And I had to accept that it would soon happen to me too.

| 29 |

On Being Frank

Great aunt Helen and her husband Frank lived a few miles outside of International Falls, off a country road. In the summer of 1953, Dad decided Diana and I could spend a couple of weeks at Aunt Helen's. We were excited with the prospect.

Helen was actually Dad's aunt, our great aunt, sister to our grandfather. She was an artist. When she was younger, she taught art at Stout, in Menomonie, Wisconsin, and now offered private painting lessons in International Falls. She also had a potter's wheel, made pots, and fired them in the walk-in kiln she had built in their backyard. In the living room she had a large floor loom where she made mostly scarves. She and a friend, Mrs. Munroe, had a little shop in downtown International Falls where they sold their pots and paintings and weavings.

Frank was a customs officer at the Canadian border between International Falls and Ft. Francis. Frank was a quiet man, crippled with arthritis, whose only passions were baseball and an aversion to hair. He looked forward to the day he could retire and move to Sarasota, Florida, where his favorite baseball team, the New York Giants, wintered and his arthritis would be better.

Helen's dad, Leslie (my great grandfather), also lived with Helen and Frank. He was senile and called me Babe. He thought I was Dad's sister, Babe.

After Dad dropped Diana and I off, the first thing Helen told us, "Never, never comb your hair or even talk about hair in Frank's presence. And especially never at the dinner table. Just the mention of hair makes Frank sick, and he'll have to leave the table."

Dinner time was lively. Great grandpa always accused Helen of trying to poison us.

"Don't eat that!" he'd yell. "She's trying to poison us all."

He didn't remember much but he probably remembered cheating Helen out of the property he promised her. Diana and I just smiled and tried to concentrate on not talking about hair.

Once, Helen had to go to the store and asked Diana and me to watch Grandpa and not let him out of the house.

"The last time I left him alone, I found him out on the road, naked, trying to flag down cars with a red shirt. He thought I abandoned him and he was going to starve to death."

Well, as soon as Helen left, Grandpa said, in desperation, "We've got to find a red flag and wave down a car! She's abandoned us and we're going to starve."

Trying to assure him, Diana said, "She'll be right back. She just went to the store."

He wasn't buying it and started going through the closets looking for something red. Finally he found a little red mothball hanger in Frank's closet.

"Babe, take this down to the road and wave down a car. Tell them to call the police," he said to me.

We said we weren't allowed to go outside and neither was he. So he stood in the big picture window facing the road and frantically waved the mothball hanger until Helen came home.

Helen and Frank slept in separate bedrooms, which I thought was strange. Diana and I slept with Helen in the back bedroom. I can't remember where Great Grandpa slept. We would have to pass through

Frank's room to get to ours. One day I accidently walked in on Frank when he was dressing, and he was stark naked! I thought I had discovered Frank's deep, dark secret. Since I had never seen a nude man before, I didn't know that men grew hair in the genital area. Also, he was a little overweight and appeared to have small breasts. I decided he must be part female and ashamed of his tell-tale pubic hair. Suddenly Frank's aversion to hair made perfect sense. I never revealed Frank's secret, not even to Diana and wondered if Helen ever knew.

Diana, Helen, and me

| 30 |

"Paul Said ...."

This was the start of every Sunday sermon at Zion Lutheran Church. And our cue to fight falling asleep.

In seventh grade, every good Lutheran started Confirmation. Confirmation classes met at church every Saturday morning, and on Sunday we were required to attend Sunday school AND church. It was a two-year commitment.

In church, we sat in the first two rows and would hear about it if we dozed off. Pastor Martin, while being the most boring speaker I've ever heard, was watching us while he droned on – for at least an hour. He loved to talk about Paul – it may have been the only stories he knew – and they had absolutely no relevance to my life. As soon as we heard those two little words it was time to daydream. This was the hardest part of Confirmation – looking like you were listening.

Up until seventh grade, church was great – we didn't go to the church service. Instead, on Sunday we attended Sunday school at 9:00 to color, listen to stories, and sing songs. While we did that, our parents attended the church service, although Dad only went to church on Easter. In the 50's, there was no adult Sunday school, so parents were ready to go home as soon as the 9:00 service was over at 10:30. Parishioners without kids usually went to the 11:00 service. Kids were never required to attend church until seventh grade and enrollment in Confirmation.

During our Saturday Confirmation class, we were randomly called on to recite the Bible verses we were supposed to have memorized during the last week.

Pastor Martin would call out a name and a verse number, "Janice, Isaiah 3:16-17."

I would stand up and recite, "Isaiah 3:16-17, The Lord said: Because the daughters of Zion are haughty and walk with outstretched necks, glancing wantonly with their eyes, mincing along as they go, tinkling with their feet; the Lord will smite with a scab the heads of the daughters of Zion, and the Lord will lay bare their secret parts."

I suppose we were told what these verses meant, but I don't remember. We were warned not to forget any of the verses because, during our final Confirmation ceremony, every one of us would be asked to recite a random verse from the last two years. He must have told us which ones he was going to ask before the big date, or I'm sure none of us would have managed to be confirmed.

Although I'm no longer a believer, I am thankful for those Confirmation years. Learning to memorize random stuff has benefited me greatly. Confirmation is also where I learned that God thought only men counted.

me sitting on Pastor Martin's left

If I had actually listened to those sermons, I might have heard Pastor Martin say, "Paul said, 'Follow me and I will make you fishers of men - just as long as you remember to throw back the women'."

| 31 |

Stories from Seventh Grade

I started seventh grade at Bryant Junior High. Several grade schools fed into Bryant, so we got to meet a lot of new kids. Entering junior high was a big, exciting step toward growing up. We were given lockers with combinations and cautioned not to share our combination with ANYONE. There were different teachers for each subject. In seventh grade, Cooking and Sewing were requirements for girls to take. For boys, it was Shop. The boys and girls took separate health/gym/swimming classes. We were responsible for our own class schedule and getting to the right class at the right time. But the best thing about junior high was the library! It was crammed with hundreds of 'real' books, not like those little picture books with childish stories that were in the Lyndale Grade School's library. I was ready for the 'real' world with stories about people.

The first day in English class, we went to the library and were told, "Pick out a book to read – any book." I went to the fiction section and picked out the biggest book I could find; it was *Jane Eyre*, and I was not disappointed. I loved the detailed descriptions of places and people and felt like I was there with Jane. There were no princesses whose only job was to be beautiful. There was no magic and no talking animals. There was only real-life problems and the promise of hope. I cried for her losses and cheered for her wins. I was just like her, or at least, wanted to be just like her. She was fearless and stood by her convictions no matter the consequences. She always did what she deemed was the right thing to do, and she was a loyal friend. Oh, what tragic figures we were. I saw in Jane that the worse the tragedy, the greater the final happiness will be. Without suffering, you don't appreciate joy.

I had a tremendous crush on my History teacher, Mr. Heaney, in seventh grade. He was so cute with his skinny neck, crew cut, and big teeth. I wrote, *A Tribute to Our Present History Teachers* and made sure it was always visible on my desk so he would see it every time he walked around the room. I was SO obnoxious too, twirling around in my hooped skirt and trying to look coquettish. I'd stare, moon-eyed and adoring, at him whenever he spoke. Once, when Mr. Heaney stepped out of the room, I climbed up on the windowsill trying to catch a butterfly. My hooped skirt went straight up in the air when I pressed against the window, exposing my underwear in all its glory, just when he came back in the room. Everyone was laughing. I wasn't particularly embarrassed, but I'm still not sure why I did that. Maybe just to make sure he noticed me.

No one ever read my gushy tribute, thank heaven. When Mr. Heaney walked around the room checking to make sure we were working on our history assignment, he always paused and looked at my tribute but never acknowledged it. I laugh every time I see the scene in *A Christmas Story* where Ralphie imagines how enraptured his teacher would be when she read his story about what he wanted for Christmas. I totally relate.

The next year Mr. Heaney didn't teach History. He only taught Shop to the boys. So I threw away my tribute.

As part of our physical education unit, we had swimming class once a week. The routine was the same, stop by the desk in the locker room and get a bathing suit. They were color coded by size and the gym teacher would look at each girl and hand her a color. No one could figure whether pink was bigger than blue, etc. and you didn't always wear the same color. I think they looked at the suits available and matched them as best they could to the students coming in. If green fit you last week, you could ask for green and, if there was one, you'd get it. The suits were wool. They stretched as soon as they got wet and hung around our knees, so size really didn't matter anyway. If we were lucky, our nipples wouldn't show.

Examples of wool bathing suits - worn by Dad's sisters, Babe and Jayne, circa 1925. I named this picture:
We never would have entered this pageant if we had known Honey Boo Boo was in it.

Before we could get in the pool, we had to go into the shower wearing the bathing suit and a swimming cap and get wet (supposedly take a shower). The first few classes consisted of putting our heads under water and learning to dog paddle. Then came jumping off the diving board; If someone wouldn't jump off the diving board, Miss Hurley would run out and push her off. We were all afraid of Miss Hurley even though she was only about four and a half feet tall and weighed about seventy-five pounds.

After class we'd shower naked, and Miss Hurley would check to make sure we used soap. We whispered about why she wanted to see us naked.

Everyone tried to get out of swimming, so I tried Athlete's Foot.

When Miss Hurley checked between my toes, she said, "Who told you that was Athlete's Foot? It's just dry skin. Get in the pool."

It turned out that I liked swimming and even became a good enough swimmer to be in the synchronized swimming group.

Girls and boys swam separately. The boys swam after the girls and they swam naked. When no one was watching, us girls would sneak behind the check-in desk before we left the locker room to look through the keyhole and see the naked boys on the diving board, which I did every chance I got. Their midsections looked pretty much the same, so you had to move your head up and down to see who you were looking at, just so you could tell the other girls who you saw naked.

Years later, at one of my high school reunions, a girl I didn't remember came up to me and said, "I remember you! You're the girl that wore undershirts and sang in the shower in junior high!"

Undershirts! Now I remember - I was the only girl wearing undershirts in my gym class.

At the time, I asked one of my friends why she was wearing a bra when she was as flat as a board.

She said, "It's a 'training' bra my Mother bought for me," and showed me how it had a pleat in it so when you do start to grow, there's room.

I realized I must be the only girl in gym class that didn't have a mother to buy me a training bra. Oh well, my undershirt had plenty of room to grow, and I'm sure it was a lot more comfortable.

Kenny had a crush on me. He was shorter than me but really cute. He had beautiful black hair and said his dad was half American Indian and half Dane. His dad was a carpenter and an alcoholic and usually gone. Kenny said his dad was over six feet tall but didn't start growing until he was eighteen, so he thought he'd probably be tall too. Kenny was the oldest of seven. His family was on welfare because his dad was mostly gone and spent his earnings on booze, or so Kenny said.

Once, I asked him where he got his moccasins.

He said, "They're my mother's slippers. I'm wearing them because I don't have any shoes that fit. I must finally be starting to grow."

Kenny's friend, Dale, was our paperboy, so Kenny started coming with him on his paper route. Dale threw the paper and Kenny threw stones at my window every morning, so I'd get up and wave at him. I appreciated the attention and imagined running out in my pajamas and kissing him. But they were always gone in a flash.

Kenny was the class clown, so I thought we would probably have a lot of fun together. But he always had a friend or two with him like he was afraid to be alone with me.

One day he said he had a funny Polaroid to show me, but it was a big secret and he didn't want anyone to know he had it. Of course he had a couple of friends with him, so we huddled together in the hall and they all anxiously watched for my reaction. Expecting to see something really funny, I already had a big smile on my face. I took the picture and turned and studied it for a while but didn't know what I was looking at.

"What is that?"

They looked at each other and, laughing, one of the boys said, "Its Karen's pussy."

My smile faded. "How did you get this? Does she know you have it?"

Karen was in my class and I knew who she was, but she wasn't a friend of mine.

Defensively, Kenny said, "Well sure. She was there, duh."

Everyone's smiles faded. Having to explain it to me was shocking to everyone and super awkward. The boys attempted teasing to lighten things back up, "You don't know what that is?" But that fell flat and we all sort of wandered off in a daze. I was embarrassed that I had never seen that and here it was a very private part of me. What could possibly be funny about it?

I'd have to give this a lot of thought. I couldn't imagine why she would let those boys take that picture and even if she did, surely she didn't know they would be showing it around school and laughing at her. It was not funny. It was cruel and humiliating. Kenny was not someone I wanted to be friends with, thus ended our budding romance. I pretended I didn't hear the rocks hit the window, and I was glad I never kissed him.

As Mother would say, "That's as funny as a rubber crutch."

I watched the Kavanaugh hearings, and it brought back memories of 'the picture.' Kavanaugh, in his hearing to become a Supreme Court Judge, dismissed Ms. Ford's allegations that he attempted to rape her thirty-six years ago, when they were in high school. His "proof" that it didn't happen was that it took her thirty-six years to come forward and how could she be sure it was even him after all those years?

It would be incredible to be told, "Maybe you forgot who showed you the picture," even though it was more than fifty years ago, or it was just a picture, all in 'fun' – not an assault. It was obvious to me our Senate is full of grown-up Kennys and his friends.

Kenny went to a different high school, so I didn't see him again until I spied him on the bus when I was nineteen. He had grown to over six feet tall and was just as cute as ever. I don't know if he recognized me, but we didn't speak.

| 32 |

Chow Mein

I love chow mein. I had it for supper five days a week for two and a half years, between fourteen and seventeen years old. My first job was working at Ranger's Chow Mein, a take-out only restaurant. It was located across the alley, on the other side of the block, from our house. I got the job (handed down to me from Diana) just before my fifteenth birthday. I made $.70 per hour. Ranger's Chow Mein was owned by our next-door neighbor, Jack Ranger. Shortly after I went to work there, Jack sold the business to his cousin, John Smith. When Jack's wife was released from the mental hospital, his housekeeper, Rene, came to work for us. Rene and the cook at Ranger's Chow Mein, Emma, were friends. I think that's how Diana got the job in the first place.

I worked from 4:00 PM to 7:00 PM Monday and Wednesday through Saturday. I missed going to the Friday football games with my friends at school, but I loved having my own spending money. I made almost $10.00 a week and mostly used my money to buy clothes and fabric. That was when I could go downtown to Three Sisters Dress Shop and buy a special dress with flocking for $12.00 ($7.50 on sale), but mostly I made my own dresses because I could make one for about $3.00.

I loved my job plus having chow mein five nights a week for supper! How great was that?

I worked with Emma, the cook, bookkeeper, and everything else, and Tom, the delivery driver and grinder/chopper operator. Tom inherited that job from his older brother. My job was taking orders, packaging the food in little square cartons, cashing the customers out, and mopping the lobby after closing.

We only saw the owner, John, when he came in to cook on Emma's occasional day off. He was big and fat and always smoked a big cigar and told dirty jokes. He told the jokes for Tom's benefit and said I shouldn't listen. But I did. Some of them were pretty funny but most of them made fun of women. Still, I liked John. When his ashes fell in the chow mein he'd say, "No one will ever notice."

Emma had a routine where she added a small amount of yesterday's left-over chow mein to each of today's batches.

"If you add too much, the starch breaks down and the chow mein is too runny."

John threw in all of yesterday's leftovers into the first batch. Usually, on his days to cook the chow mein wasn't so good, especially the first batch.

When I got to work, I went into the basement to change into my uniform, a stiffly starched, heavy white cotton dress that hung almost to the floor. I tied on my little white apron to give me a waist. Once a month the exterminator came to spray for bugs. On the days he sprayed, Emma would warn me not to turn on the lights in the basement or to change in the walk-in cooler. Usually I chose the walk-in cooler because the basement floor would be covered with hundreds of dead and dying large roach bodies, and I sure didn't want to be stepping on them or seeing them. That night, after everyone left, Emma would go down and sweep the bodies up.

I always hated to open a new box of noodles because, a lot of the time, when I stuck my hand in the new box, a bug or two would come running out, sometimes up my arm.

I jumped back, "Jeez! A roach just ran over my hand!"

"They won't hurt you. And they aren't roaches. They're water bugs," Emma would say.

That made it better, I guess, but I wondered why water bugs would be in a box of dry chow mein noodles.

John bought his supplies from Mr. Chang, whose business was periodically closed by the health department. Emma would order ahead of time just in case a shipment was delayed.

"Why don't we just buy things from someone else?"

"John keeps him because Mr. Chang is so much cheaper than all the other suppliers," Emma said.

In tenth grade, my Home Economics teacher asked me about the restaurant. She was considering buying chow mein occasionally for her family and wanted to make sure the restaurant was really clean.

"It's really clean and the chow mein is really good. I eat it every night for supper. When you come in, I'll show you the kitchen and you can meet Emma, the cook."

I left out the parts about the water bugs in the noodles and the cigar ashes in the chow mein and crunchy roaches in the basement and how one time Tom cut off the tip of his finger in the food chopper/grinder when he was chopping the celery. The finger wasn't important anyway. Emma made Tom rewash the celery after he fished out his fingertip and bandaged his hand.

My teacher visited and inspected the woks and the range hoods and the steam table and bought some chow mein. I don't remember that she ever came back.

Ranger's is where I met my first boyfriend, Tom (the boy without a fingertip). Other than walking me home from work, I don't remember what we did on our dates except ride around in his family car whenever he could get it. Tom's best friend, Tom (with a broken, crooked nose), worked as a delivery boy at the Garden Grocery & Meat Market next door to Ranger's Chow Mein. After Tom and I decided we were going steady, he asked me to fix up his friend, Tom (with the broken nose). I fixed Tom up with my friend, Betty, and we double-dated. Tom and Betty lasted a lot longer than Tom (without the fingertip) and me.

I liked talking to Emma. She talked to me as a friend and an adult. When I complained about my dad (which I did often and to anyone who would listen) she never tried to tell me I was wrong and needed to be grateful (something every other adult felt compelled to say).

Once I told her about a kitten I found but lost again. It was in the fall and I spent my evenings hunting for it because I was afraid it would freeze to death.

One really cold night, Rene said, "Emma called and said she found your kitten. It's on her porch and you need to go over there and get it right away."

I brought it home and pretended it was really the kitten I had lost. I didn't want to hurt their feelings. And this kitten needed a home too. I called him Cat, the same as the other kitten.

Ranger's is also where I received some valuable insight into my relationship with my dad.

Emma confided in me, "Rene told me your dad said the reason he was so strict with you and not your sisters and brother was because you are so much like your mother. He's afraid you have inherited your mother's genes that made her have her nervous breakdown."

At the time, it was widely believed that mental illness was inherited. The jury is still out on that.

Strangely, it was comforting. Now I could stop wondering what was so terrible about me and how I could fix it. Now I could ignore Dad without feeling guilty or inadequate. I was empowered. If Mother was crazy, I was okay with being crazy too. I loved her just the way she was.

| 33 |

Chartreuse

In the summer after tenth grade, I asked my mother what she wanted for her birthday in August.

She said, "I'd really like a pair of chartreuse corduroy slacks. I don't have any nice clothes."

I bought some beautiful, deep rosy red corduroy material and made the pants. I made a perfect bound buttonhole and the zipper was perfectly installed. The pockets were satin and done just right. I was smugly proud of my work and asked my uncle Pat to drive me to St. Peter to see Mother on her birthday.

When she opened the package, she gave me a half-smile and said, "Thank you."

"Isn't that what you wanted?"

"I wanted chartreuse and I don't really like pink."

"That's not chartreuse?"

Pat said, "No, chartreuse is an ugly pea green. These are much prettier."

But I knew what Mother was thinking.

Even my own daughter thinks it is okay to second-guess what I really want.

That's what I would have thought. I was so sorry I disappointed her.

Chartreuse, Magenta. Why not yellow-green, bright pink? Or day-glow green, day-glow pink? Well, at least I will never forget what color chartreuse is.

| 34 |

Cars

My boyfriend, Tom, (and all the boys) talked endlessly about cars. They could recognize all the makes and models.

I questioned, "What's so interesting about cars that you have to memorize every make, model, and year?"

Disgusted at my ignorance, Tom said, "It's a GUY thing. Girls could never learn to recognize the different makes and models and years."

I had to take the challenge, even though I thought it was just a useless, boring waste of time. The next few weeks I actually looked at every car, making a mental note of the make and model and asking what year it was. I soon figured out that each make had certain characteristics that persisted through the years, each model was in a hierarchy by price (the more chrome the pricier the car), and every year all the cars for that year had certain similarities. Then I could look at a car I'd never seen and pretty accurately extrapolate the make, model, and year. Tom was impressed and so were his friends. From this, I earned the reputation of being smart (for a girl). Although I was suddenly brainy, it didn't help my popularity with the boys. Brainy wasn't a desirable attribute for a girlfriend. But I didn't care; those memorization skills from Confirmation were paying off.

| 35 |

Irene's Story

At the beginning of my junior year in high school, I was told I could take an English elective instead of regular English. I liked diagramming sentences and punctuation, grammar, and spelling were so easy. The elective English offerings were things like American Literature and Public Speaking. Because I had a terrible fear of getting up in front of the class to speak and it affected the grades in all my classes, I signed up for Public Speaking, hoping to overcome my fear. I had visions of a room full of students just like me who needed pointers and encouragement to get over their fear of public speaking. But it wasn't like that. On day one, we were given a schedule of upcoming debates to prepare for. And a pep talk about how we were going to blow the socks off the competition. I knew right away this class wasn't what I was hoping for, but still, surely when the teacher saw how bad off I was, she'd guide me through it. Wrong again. I would prepare my speeches but when I'd get up in front of the class, my face would turn red and my eyes would tear up and my mind would go blank, just like I knew I would. Instead of help, the teacher would angrily tell me to sit down.

Then came her ready lecture - "I'm tired of you coming to my class every day unprepared. If you took this class because you thought it would be easy, you're sadly mistaken. If you don't start putting some effort into this class, I'll fail you."

No use in trying to defend myself. I wasn't willing to demean myself in front of the class any more than I already had.

One day, Irene, one of the girls in my circle of friends, said she had to write a story for her English class and she was panicking. She couldn't do it and begged me to do it for her. I thought it was a great assignment and was happy to write it.

I wrote a very scary story about a girl in peril and, at the end, she was hanging on for dear life to a post covered in barbed wire. She woke up and found she was lying on her bedroom floor and hanging on to her mother's "briar-patch" leg. (That's what we used to call it when we didn't shave our legs often enough.)

After Irene got her grade (an A+), she ran up and gave me an enthusiastic cheerleaderly hug. She was so excited she couldn't stop talking and laughing. Her teacher told her she should become a writer! And now Irene was sure she was the teacher's pet. She gushed her thanks all over me. I wasn't so happy.

Irene made an A in her English class and went on to be homecoming queen; I made an F in Public Speaking and got to go to summer school. In summer school, our assignment was to read *The Old Man and the Sea* during class, discuss the deeper meaning of the story and then write a book report. My report was so long I decided to present it in book form with a collage featuring the old man's struggle on the cover.

The summer school teacher asked, "Exactly why are you in summer school English?"

"I took Public Speaking and I was lousy at it."

I think the lessons learned in summer school were more valuable than making the debate team. From the old man I learned that the things I work at are part of my identity (not Irene's). What redeems my life from being meaningless is using my skills, being passionate about what I do, accepting my failures with dignity, fighting off the sharks, and passing on what I can (while never doing someone else's work).

From the summer school teacher I learned that stories are not just what's written down but what's there between the lines. He gave me an A which translated into a C in Public Speaking for the record. Fear of public speaking is still with me. And no matter what, I would have never been a homecoming queen. That is who Irene was.

| 36 |

Dad's Divorce

After Mother had been in and out the mental hospital for eleven years, Dad obtained a divorce on the grounds that if someone was in a mental hospital for at least five years they were considered incurably insane, and this was grounds for divorce in Minnesota.

He told us, "Your mother is never going to be well and never going to come home for good. We need to move on so I'm divorcing her."

Fortunately for Dad, there would be no question of custody, no child support, no alimony, and no one to contest. After all, she was legally insane. This divorce also meant Mother could never be released. She no longer had a guardian. Dr. Stein apparently had planned to release Mother once again until consulting with Dad. If Mother was released before the divorce was final, the divorce would not be granted. Mother would no longer be incurably insane. So, she languished in the mental hospital for another four years.

Mother's response to Dad's request for divorce:

February 24, 1958 - Dear Les, I just asked Dr. Stien when he planned to release me in March. He denied he had said anything about my going in March, but said he is waiting for a visit from you before he releases me. You don't have to worry about our past marriage. I am practically engaged to Floyd Oamodt. Stien is a Catholic and they don't believe in divorce. Nuts to them. I at first, wished you weren't divorcing me but when Pa, Ethel & Dr. Grimes got thru talking to me I rather agreed to it. I still think it's too bad that had to happen as we certainly got along before my nervous breakdown and all. Oh well, "let by-gones just be by-gones." Sincerely, Millie

| 37 |

Jim

At sixteen, I desperately needed to talk to Mother about boys and sex and marriage. She was the only person I could/would talk to about those things. But Dad had divorced Mother so she could never come home again and I had no access to her. I didn't have a driver's license or a car, she couldn't accept phone calls, and all her mail was censored. So, I relied on movies to inform me about these things. Unfortunately, movies in the '50s were mostly produced by misogynist pricks. The gorgeous, whining, crying, empty-headed, powerless, groveling women of the movies were lousy role models. I knew I could never compete with their looks but certainly having a usable brain should count for something. With all the terrible things that happened to Mother, she never groveled.

On the other hand, most of the men in the movies were wonderful. Cary Grant was the one for me. I imagined, one day, when I was in my 20s and independent, I would be walking down the street and probably trip and maybe accidently fall in an open man-hole. Cary (or someone that looked just like him) would be the only person to see this and rush to rescue me. When he pulled me out, I'd notice he had ripped his perfectly fitting suit.

I'd say, "Oh, I'm so sorry. Let me fix that for you. I can mend it so you will never know it was torn."

While he waited, in his underwear, we'd talk and he'd fall madly in love with me. He'd beg me to marry him and have his children.

Then there was Jim. During the spring of my junior year, before I ran away to Florida, Jim and I dated. He was a year older than I was, a senior, and ran with the "bad boys" (Fonzie or James Dean types), - the popular crowd. Jim was the youngest of seven and all his siblings were alcoholics. He said his father died when he was young and was also an alcoholic who abused his mother. Charlotte was a sweet, lovely woman and we spent a lot of time with her. Jim wanted to take care of his mother and said he would never let himself become an alcoholic like his father or brothers.

When Jim graduated from high school, he and some of his friends joined the Marines and were sent to Vietnam. That summer, when I ran away to Florida, I didn't give any thought to the fact that we would probably never see each other again. After all, he was only a placeholder until Cary came along to rescue me from a manhole.

| 38 |

The Runaway

Dad's go-to form of punishment was to send me to my room. I was sent to my room whenever I did or said something he didn't like, which was almost everything I did or said.

"Go to your room!"

I'd give him a defiant look and stamp up the stairs.

On my way up he'd yell after me, "If you don't like it here, find somewhere else to live!"

After a pause, he'd follow it with, "But no one would have you."

I spent a lot of my teenage years in my room, but that wasn't all bad. I'm not a very spontaneous person and like to always have a plan. Alone in my room, I made plans. Or maybe it was more like plotting, but I put the time to good use.

I was resigned to the status quo with Dad, so I decided I would live with my great-aunt Helen in Sarasota, Florida, although I neglected to inform her. When Diana and I used to visit her in International Falls, she seemed to like having us there. I even went up to visit her alone a couple of times.

So, Helen it was. I wrote and said I'd like to come for a visit when school was out for summer break. I found out how much a bus ticket was to Sarasota and since I had a job, I had the means to save enough for a round-trip ticket. I didn't think Dad would let me go if I only bought a one-way ticket. He would figure out what my intentions were and wouldn't let me go.

When school was out at the end of my junior year and I had finished summer school, I was on my way! The bus trip in itself was an adventure. The farthest I'd been from home until that point was when we visited Helen and walked across the border to Ft. Francis, Alberta, Canada so Helen could buy Canadian bacon.

On the bus, while passing through Kentucky during the night, we picked up a scrawny man, probably in his twenties, carrying a guitar. He looked around the bus and headed right for the seat next to me.

"I'm on my way to boot camp in Ft. Hood TX. I'm going to the same camp where Elvis is and plan to meet him. I'm a country-western singer like Elvis."

He proceeded to grab my arm and put his head on my shoulder and began singing, "Send Me Your Pillow to Dream On," loudly, while playing his guitar. He woke up everyone on the bus and while they all watched us, he begged me to send him my pillow. That was the first uncomfortable part of the trip. I kept looking at the bus driver in his rear-view mirror, hoping he would do something, but he didn't. He was watching us though, just like everyone else on the bus. Fortunately, my serenader transferred to another bus in Alabama, but not before he gave me his name and address and got a promise from me that I would really send him my pillow. I threw it away at the next stop. Now I wish I could remember his name. Did Jerry Lee Lewis go into the Army at Ft. Hood in 1958?

When I got to the southern states on the bus, I started to see "Whites Only" signs on the drinking fountains, rest rooms, and even at the lunch counters. Having gone to Central High where about a quarter of the student body was African American, it felt like I was going back to a scary time in a long-ago history. It was the second uncomfortable part of the trip.

When I stepped off the bus in Sarasota, my first words to Helen were, "Is it okay if I live with you?" No sense in beating around the bush.

"Have you talked to your dad? Is it okay with him?"

"I'm sure it is. He keeps telling me to find another place to live."

Then I went to the window at the Greyhound station and cashed in my return ticket.

The summer was okay but there wasn't much to do. Helen introduced me to all her old art students and old teachers and old neighbors. Everyone I met was old. Never having children, she worried too much about her "responsibility" and didn't want me going off on my own. Helen painted a few pictures of me, but she thought I was too pale. I tried lying out in the sun and Helen painted me on the chaise lounge, but it was too hot and I only burned. Plus, it was boring and lying in the sun made me nauseous.

Before I left home, Betty and Tom (Tom with the broken nose) introduced me to their friend, Moose whose family was moving to St. Petersburg, Florida. Moose would drive down most weekends and we'd go out to a movie or to the beach. He wasn't very interesting and not very bright, but I appreciated having a "boyfriend." I wished I had a job but there was nothing within walking distance.

Helen had a new gadget she was proud of – a microwave! I'd never seen one and don't think I'd ever heard of them. I didn't think they'd ever catch on. And what difference did it make if it took two minutes to boil water in the microwave or three in a saucepan?

I was glad to enroll in school in the fall and made a few friends, but I was beginning to rethink the wisdom of this move. The big thing kids did here was to walk up and down the beach in the hot sand and get sunburned.

My English teacher asked if I'd read Shakespeare last year at school and I hadn't. I guess if I hadn't wasted my time in Public Speaking last year, I would have read Shakespeare. She said they had studied it last year and this year it would be all about analyzing Shakespeare.

"Since you haven't read it, you won't know what we're talking about, and I don't have the time to go over it with you, so you don't need to participate. You don't even need to come to class. I'll give you an A."

What a deal! I showed up to class anyway because I had nothing better to do. But I really didn't know what they were talking about.

I signed up for Chemistry and was looking forward to it, but the chemistry teacher didn't want to teach it – she was a coach and not interested in teaching chemistry. Every day she'd show up for the first 15 minutes of class. She'd take attendance and we'd go over our supply list and verify that we had all our beakers, chemicals, and charts. Then she'd leave. We were on our own until the bell rang.

I made a few friends, mostly just Sharon. Sharon's dad was a Presbyterian minister and I often spent the night at her house on weekends. They did a lot of praying but otherwise acted normal and quite nice. Sharon's parents let her use the family car whenever she wanted so we spent a lot of time driving to the beach and just driving around.

Southern culture was a little different than I was familiar with. Lots of the girls were engaged to older guys, and Sharon was engaged to a sailor. It seemed like a girl must have something wrong with her if she wasn't engaged before she got out of high school. Back in Minnesota, I didn't know a single person who was engaged in high school. A few accidently got pregnant and married but never engaged.

Towards the end of the first grading period, Helen said, "I talked to your Dad and he thinks you need to come home."

Secretly, I was relieved. He sent the money for my bus trip home, and he stopped sending me to my room and never told me to live somewhere else again, but he never told me he was glad to have me back either.

My old life with my siblings and friends was good to have back though, and I got a job as a carhop at Curran's Drive In with my friend, Kay. The best part was that it would be only nine months until I could get an adult job and move into an apartment.

My new chemistry teacher told me they had already memorized the periodic table and said if I didn't have it memorized immediately, I'd have to drop chemistry. So I memorized the periodic table. Once again, those memorization skills from Confirmation were paying off. I loved chemistry and thought I'd like to become a chemist and save the world through the magic of chemistry. Or maybe plate everything I owned in silver.

| 39 |

Jim Returns

I had promised Jim I'd write while he was away, had a lot of fun with that, and wrote once or twice a week through the summer and into the fall. My letters were very newsy, and Jim said everyone in his barracks looked forward to them. I remember one of my letters was about my friend Kay when she had Trench Mouth. The doctor said, "Trench Mouth causes your gums to recede and if you hadn't come in, all your teeth would have fallen out." So much fodder to speculate about how she might have contracted it and what she would do with her teeth when they all fell out. I called it Hoof and Mouth Disease. Jim's letters were more romantic. I'd send him little gifts and once I sent him a pair of undershorts I had made from red heart fabric. Jim said he wore them around the base instead of his outer shorts.

In December, Jim said he was coming home on leave and bringing me a ring. I was so worried it was an engagement ring and didn't know how I would refuse it without hurting his feelings. I was relieved when he gave me a pretty ring with three pearls, three diamonds and little gold fans on either side. He said it was a cocktail ring.

Jim wearing red heart underwear in Vietnam

He invited me to a party with his friends. I noticed Jim was drinking a lot and seemed drunk most of the time. I thought maybe he was just excited to be home on leave. Besides, I liked to drink (one beer was all I could manage) and didn't see it as a problem. When I was drinking, I thought I was the funniest person alive.

At the party Jim said, "Let's go out to the car and make out." I was all for it.

In the car, he unbuttoned my blouse. I had on a beautiful, new, cobalt blue slip. It was in his way and he just ripped it open down the middle, breaking a strap, and pulling it out one of my sleeves. I was stunned. I can't remember doing anything to stop him. Next, Jim unzipped his pants and shoved my face in his lap. He held my head there and gave me instructions. When it was over, I went in the house to the bathroom to wash my mouth out. Once in the bathroom, I started to cry.

I noticed that several of the girls followed me upstairs. None of them were friends of mine but they seemed to know what had happened and said things like, "Don't take it so hard. He was just having fun."

When I started down the stairs, there was Jim, waving my torn slip in the air and all the guys were laughing and cheering. I just stood there, shocked as it dawned on me that everyone knew what was going to happen when we went to the car. It wasn't just Jim that humiliated, demeaned, and assaulted me. It was all his friends too. I wanted to run and hide but stood frozen while processing what was happening. Then

I thought, *I don't need or want friends like these. I don't belong here, and I don't have to accept this humiliation.*

I grabbed my slip from his hand and said, "Take me home - now."

"But the party just got started."

"Then I'll call a cab."

I lived at least twenty miles away and had no idea how I would pay for the cab. I couldn't ask my dad for the money because I would have to tell him at least a version of what happened, and he'd tell me it was my own fault. And how did I intend to pay him back for the cab ride? Fortunately, Jim agreed to take me home. In the car, he tried to laugh off the incident.

By now, I had recovered enough to be raging mad. "Don't EVER call me again."

"If you're going to break up with me, I may as well kill us both. I'll drive this car off a cliff or drive it into the Mississippi." He was really drunk. "You don't think I will? Just watch me."

I could never revert to simpering and whining, so calling his bluff was my only option. "Just do it then."

Besides, there were no cliffs along Portland Avenue, and I couldn't think of a single place where a car could get close enough to the river to drive it in. *You dumb shit.*

He begged me to reconsider breaking up and finally said he was sorry. But I don't think he understood why he should be sorry. Then I was home, and I hid my once beautiful blue slip in the trash. I laid awake all night thinking about my anger, my humiliation, and my shame.

| 40 |

The Transom

Several years ago, in 1982, my brother Steve called to tell me he just left an auction of the contents of my old high school, Central High, in Minneapolis. It was being torn down.

He said, "I almost bought one of the transoms from a classroom, but I didn't."

Of all the things that must have been auctioned off, that was the one thing I would have wanted. It was a reminder of my first true love.

Clarence was in Art with me in the spring of our senior year in high school. We sat next to each other and became Art Class friends. I was impressed with his artistic talent. His work was impressionistic and emotional - talent I didn't possess.

Art was the last class of the day on Friday. I was working in the back room on an art project when the bell rang, but I wanted to finish what I was doing, so I didn't leave. When I finished, the door was locked, and everyone was gone. Being inventive, I put a table in front of the door and a chair on the table and thought I could climb out the transom, eight feet up. I pulled myself up and realized there wasn't enough room to turn around. The only way out would be to drop down on my head. I couldn't go back because I couldn't look back to see the chair and if I knocked it over on the table as I slid back, I'd fall and land on the overturned chair, then on the floor. That would hurt. If the chair fell off the table when it overturned and I landed on the bare table, I'd still fall off the table and then land in the overturned chair. I wasn't willing to take the risk that the chair wouldn't overturn so there I hung, trying to think of another option when Clarence came by.

"Hi, Clarence. I'm stuck."

Surprised, he looked up to see where the voice was coming from.

"I guess you are (ha ha). How did you get there anyway?"

"I'm so glad you came along! I was locked in and didn't want to spend the weekend in the art room. This wasn't such a good idea, and now I'm stuck up here."

"Drop down and I'll catch you."

So I did. I dropped out of the transom headfirst and he caught me. Then he walked me home from school.

I liked Clarence for a long time but knew he was out of my league. He was gorgeous, captain of the football team, the basketball team, and the track team. He was tall and graceful and had an absolutely gorgeous body. Add to that, he even had a beautiful smile and long beautiful fingers. Of course he had a large following of female admirers. He was also kind, smart, funny, and mature. I was secretly thrilled when he walked me home from school. Maybe it showed. He started walking me home every day he didn't have practice, and I was in love.

At home, we no longer had a housekeeper so it was only me, Linda fifteen, and Steve, eleven, at home after school. Clarence would stay for a while but Linda and Steve would always be right there to pull up a chair and join in. They wanted to hear all about school sports. It irritated me; I wanted to be alone with him, but Clarence enjoyed it.

Pat and Jerry from the Garden Grocery eventually told Dad they saw a colored boy walking me home several times.

Dad said, "You're not allowed to have boys in the house when I'm not home."

I don't think Dad was racist, but he worried a lot about what other people thought so that had to be the extent of his rule. So Clarence walked me home and we sat on the front porch.

When I asked Clarence if he was going to college, he said he was offered a football scholarship to Carlton, but he didn't take it because he didn't want to play football. He was a better basketball player and loved track. He saw himself as the tackle dummy for the huge football players at Carlton. He would last about one year before he'd be out with injuries, no degree, and no future. He didn't know what he was going to do.

Before and after graduation, Clarence called almost every night, and we would meet on the corner, always after dark, and walk down to Lake Calhoun or Lake Harriet. We'd sit on the beach, and sometimes the lawn of the Greek Orthodox Church, to talk and make out. Did I say I was in love? He was perfect – my Cary Grant. And I didn't have to fall in a manhole. Of course, being stuck in a transom was kind of similar; I still had to be rescued but unlike Cary, Clarence never proposed.

Clarence wrote in my yearbook, "Until the twelfth of never, I'll still be loving you."

He gave me a 5 x 7 of his graduation picture and wrote, "If things were different, you know what I would do."

One night while we were walking to the lake, some boys in a car yelled, "N--r lover!"

I started to run after them so I could see who they were, but Clarence stopped me and said, "Just ignore them."

I was pretty sure I'd know them; they were cruising in my neighborhood, and I wanted to see their faces. It was a verbal fight I wanted, but Clarence must have known it would morph into a chance for four or five guys to beat the shit out of him.

When he dropped me back at the house that night, he repeated what he'd written on his picture, "If things were different, you know what I would do." And he quit calling.

I knew my place in the world - I was just a woman. Clarence lifted me up. He thought I was special. I will always love him for that. Naively I thought with all his talents and the fact that he was male he had it all and would always be a star; nothing could stop him. I also knew he would eventually leave me for one of his many other female admirers because an interracial romance would be too problematic for him. For me, it didn't seem like much of a problem. Being just a woman, no one expected much from me. Besides, conflict was my middle name. I couldn't and didn't expect Clarence to want this fight.

| 41 |

My Blue Bathing Suit

I was reading what everyone wrote in my final (1959) yearbook and noticed that almost every boy that signed it mentioned they were looking forward to seeing me at the beach. At first, I couldn't figure out why, since I didn't go very often to the beach. Lying in the sun made me feel sick, and shaving my legs from top to bottom was such a chore. Then I remembered my blue bathing suit from last summer. It was two-piece and I made it myself. It fit like a glove.

The conventional wisdom of the time was that the measurements for the perfect body were - hips and bust had to be the same (preferably thirty-six inches each) and the waist had to be ten inches smaller (twenty-six inches). My measurements were thirty-one and a half, eighteen, and thirty-six. At least one of my measurements was good. I couldn't do anything about my too small waist but I could make a bathing suit that would fix everything. I bought the thickest foam rubber 'falsies' I could find and sewed them into the bra. My suit was completely lined, so there was no way to get even a glimpse of the falsies. I never admitted they were there, not even to my best friends.

At the beach, boys would accidently bump into me in order to feel whether they were real, as if they would know the difference. I think I had them all fooled and I had almost perfect measurements.

| 42 |

Looking For Sailors

Kay and I were friends in high school, and we were both carhops at Curran's Drive-In. Kay was the oldest of eight with a sometimes-abusive, alcoholic father. We both wanted to get away from home, so the summer after graduation, we got an apartment together. Kay got a job at NW Bell as a long-distance operator, and I found an office job with Barber Oil, keeping track of inventory and helping with accounts payable. Kay and her brother Kenny bought a Nash Metropolitan. They loved that car.

After about a year, we decided to change our living arrangements. Kay moved in with three other girls she worked with, and I moved in with Beth, a girl I worked with. Sandy, one of Kay's new roommates, said sailors would be coming into port in Chicago in a couple of weeks. We decided to go to Chicago to meet some sailors. We loved their cute white uniforms and thought it would be romantic to have a sailor for a boyfriend. The three of us headed for Chicago in Kay's little Metropolitan, and we rented a room in an ancient downtown Chicago hotel. We asked the hotel employees and people on the elevated where the sailors were, but no one seemed to know what we were talking about. We never found the sailors but had a good time anyway riding all over Chicago on the elevated and looking for sailors.

Since we all had to be home for work on Monday morning, we decided to drive all night on Sunday. My driving turn came at 4:00 AM. I wasn't at all used to being up at that time. My eyes were wide open, but my brain wasn't. About 6:00 AM I saw construction warning signs, SLOW – CONSTRUCTION ZONE then, SLOW – SHARP TURN AHEAD with a big arrow pointing left. My eyes saw it but not my brain. I didn't slow down, and I didn't even attempt to make the turn. We shot straight off the highway and the little Metropolitan landed in a big pile of sand, sinking to the running boards! The sun was coming up and construction workers were just arriving at work when we landed right in their midst. I turned off the car but I'm not sure it was even running. Then I just sat there, figuring out what just happened as my brain came to life. Kay and Sandy had been asleep.

"Ow!"

"Ow! What happened?"

Kay bumped her head, Sandy was wedged on the floor in the back, and I bumped my knee on the dashboard and my nose on the steering wheel. Heads started to appear, and we looked like a clown car coming to life.

The workers stood around our car peering in at us and laughing. "Are you alright?"

Rolling down the windows, we all three chimed, "I think so," and stumbled out of the car.

After some discussion, the crew decided they could probably all together lift that little car, and they did! They picked it out of the sand and set the car back on the road. We thanked them profusely, got back in the car, waved good-bye, and off we went. When we got home, I noticed that the frame was sprung. I said nothing and maybe Kay didn't notice but for the rest of the time Kay owned her little Metropolitan it went down the road with the chassis facing left at a 20-degree angle from the frame.

| 43 |

Kay's Wedding Dress

Even after Kay and I went to work full time, we kept our carhop jobs at Curran's Drive-In. I saved enough money to buy a car, a 1956 Pontiac Bonneville, and Kay helped me get my driver's license.

Kay soon began dating Sandy's brother, and, before long, they were engaged. Jim was in college and worked the summers with his family in the carnival business. Kay got in the habit of running away every time they had a fight. Then she'd call me from the Walgreen's on the corner of Hennepin and Lake and want me to pick her up.

"Come and get me! We had a fight, and I can't go home! I don't know what to do!"

Of course, I always dropped what I was doing and picked her up. This freaked Jim out every time, and he'd be out hunting for her all night. When Kay would call him in the morning, he'd beg her to come back.

Finally, he said, "Kay, you need to stop associating with Janice. She's a bad influence on you. You wouldn't run away if she wouldn't come and get you."

Kay pretty much ignored him on this. And Jim continued to blame me every time Kay ran away.

Kay wanted me to make her wedding dress, and I was happy to do it. Not having enough money to buy tons of material for a long dress with a train, we decided on a short dress, above the knees.

"Kay, you have great legs. You should show them off," I told her.

We bought white curtain material covered with embossed white roses, looking almost like raw silk covered in lace. The dress had long sleeves with 6 satin buttons and looped closures on each sleeve and the same buttons and closures down the back of the dress. It had a high neck and a full skirt with lots of net slips underneath and a white velvet cummerbund. She looked great – almost like a ballerina. She was a beautiful bride, and everyone told her so. But after the wedding, one of Jim's aunts said the dress made her "look cheap" because it was so short.

Jim was quick to remark, "That was Janice. It was her idea to make the dress so short."

I was peeved at Kay for not coming to my defense, but I shouldn't have been. After all, it was her day and a negative remark by someone that I knew didn't like me didn't come close to equating to wrecking her car.

Later Kay said Jim's aunt was "crazy" and she loved the dress. After the wedding, we didn't keep in touch. I forgot to tell her I was sorry for wrecking her car but I am. Truly, good friends are forever.

| 44 |

Judy

My new roommate Beth and I had another roommate, Judy, and we shared a one-bedroom upper duplex. Pretty soon Beth decided it was too crowded and moved out. I think that was what she had in mind all along. She moved in with her cooler friends. That was fine because I really liked Judy. She was the sweetest, nicest person in the world and had a great sense of humor. She just didn't know what a great person she was.

Judy's greatest ambition was to get married and have children. Myself, I thought I wasn't old enough to get married, and I sure wasn't ready to enslave myself to some man. Now that I had a car, I was saving my money to go to college and become a chemist.

Judy had false teeth (she said) but slept with them in. She "would die" if anyone saw her without her teeth – even her future husband, Al. I didn't much like Al. He wasn't good enough for Judy. Al was not a kind or insightful person, and it was always his way or the highway. Judy was expected to wait on him; plus, he didn't have a sense of humor. But she was so happy that he was willing to marry her. Al wanted to wait to get married until they had saved enough for a down-payment on a house. I suspect Judy was the one seriously saving every penny she could. I told Judy she was too good for him, and she thought I was too good for Jerry.

Judy ironed everything, even her underwear, and hung them on hangers. Her closet was jam packed. Judy had a hope chest where she kept all the things she was saving for her marriage, including a frilly nightgown for her wedding night. It was pink with a rayon undergarment and covered by a ruffley, sheer outer layer. It had a built-in bra (to make her look bigger busted) and lots of pink paper flowers sewed to one corner of the bra. I liked to tease her, especially about her wedding night in her pink negligee.

"Why didn't you wait to buy that until just before you got married?" (I thought it was God-awful ugly but never said that.)

Judy laughed. "I probably should have waited but it was just what I dreamed of and it was on sale. But it looks like by the time Al is ready to get married, it will probably be rotten and fall apart when I put it on."

Clarence called and asked if he could borrow ten dollars. I said, "Sure." and gave him the money. A few weeks later he called again and wanted twenty dollars.

I said, "I don't have twenty dollars to spare."

"I'll call your Dad and all your friends and tell them we had a thing going if you don't give me the money."

I was hurt and said, "Go ahead. I'm not embarrassed about that and if they are, that's their problem."

He hung up and never called again.

| 45 |

Jerry

Betty and Tom introduced me to Jerry, a college friend of Tom's, and we started dating. They thought Jerry and I would make a good couple because they thought we were both smart and artistic. Tom met Jerry at the University of Minnesota. Jerry thought he wanted to be an engineer but dropped out after the first year and went to the Minneapolis School of Art instead.

The summer after we started dating, Jerry's dad got him a summer job working in the warehouse at Barber Oil, where I worked. We started dating more frequently and having sex. I was counting days and naive. Birth control pills hadn't been invented.

In February, on my birthday as far as I can figure, Jerry took me out for my birthday, and we had sex. I got pregnant. I thought I had ulcers and went to the doctor. He said I was pregnant.

I told Judy and she cried. "Why couldn't it have been me? I'm the one that wants a baby."

When I told Jerry, he cried and asked, "What are you going to do?"

So, then I knew I was on my own. There was no *we* in his mind.

I was scared and, for the first time in my life, I couldn't imagine what I would do next. I didn't have a plan. Once again, I needed my mother. But I couldn't upset her with this news. She had just gotten released from the hospital and I was afraid if she got too worked up about this, someone would dump her back in the hospital.

I first waited for Jerry to man up, but he didn't do it. While this was going on, his younger sister Jean had become pregnant, waited until her parents went on vacation, and took out a marriage license (in Minnesota, there's a three-day wait and a required publishing of the license request in the paper). Friends of her parents saw the notice and called them. They rushed home to stop the marriage. They insisted she had only two options: go to live with her sister in California and give the baby up for adoption or be disowned by the family. Jean's boyfriend was the villain, and they wanted him charged with rape. She chose door number two, got married and dropped out of college. All this traumatized Jerry. He thought his parents would treat him like they treated Jean's boyfriend, and more importantly, stop paying for his college and take away his car. For Jerry, standing up to his parents was unthinkable. His dad was still taking him shopping for his clothes, owned his car and all his "toys" and paid for his education – and reminded him often.

I thought it was just his excuse to avoid any responsibility. Maybe he was incapable of standing on his own, and, if that was the case, I didn't want him in my life. I was on my own, and I didn't want to be married to a self-centered coward. I needed an adult. Too bad this was the way I would come to realize that.

| 46 |

Illegitimate

What was I going to do? There were no legal abortions but there should have been. I don't know whether I would have had one but I very much resent that I didn't have the option. It was my life, my future – not some stranger's choice to make. That left me with public shame for me AND my child or giving my child to some strangers and having faith that they would be good parents; the same group of strangers that thought they should impose their moral values on me. I couldn't trust them. So my only option was to have my baby and raise it. I felt bad for the hardships I was imposing on my child but resolved to be the best mother I could be.

I went to Human Services and they said I could go through Lutheran or Catholic Charities to have my baby. The Lutheran Charities' home for unwed mothers was in Minneapolis and the Catholic Charities' home for unwed mothers was in St. Paul. In either place I would be required to spend the last 6 weeks of my pregnancy living at the home. Most, if not all the younger girls spent their entire pregnancy there – hiding. If I chose not to spend the entire time there, Lutheran Charities and Catholic Charities would find me employment as a mother's helper in a Lutheran home/Catholic home. I would be paid $15.00 per week. I chose this route. First I talked with Lutheran Charities, and they had a family I could work for. It was across the street from Jerry's family! So I chose Catholic because it was in St. Paul, and there was less of a chance that anyone I knew would see me there.

While I was navigating my new reality, Jim was discharged from the Marines. Out of the blue he called me and wanted to go out.

I said, "I'm pregnant and leaving town."

I thought that would end any further interest, but Jim wanted to talk more about my predicament. He said he wanted to marry me. *He hardly knew me. We hadn't talked or corresponded since that awful party.*

He said, "We can get married. I'll rejoin the Marines and we'd go wherever that takes us."

"I'll think about it and call you after I have the baby."

I knew I didn't love him – probably didn't even like him - and the memory of that party still seared my brain, but it was a way to be respectable again and give my child a father, albeit an alcoholic one.

In the months before I entered the home, I worked for a couple in St. Paul, Mary and Angelo, and did the cleaning, laundry, shopping, and usually made dinner. The couple had two children (John, 2, and Mary, 4) who Mary took care of. Mary's mother also lived there. She had a stroke and was bed ridden and whined all day about how no one loved her or called or came to visit her any more. She had two sons and her daughter, Mary. Of course the family had decided Mary had to be the caretaker since she was the only daughter and didn't work. Her mother refused to go into a nursing home and would sob and accuse Mary of not loving her if the topic was even mentioned. Mary's brothers and sisters-in-law never bothered to call or visit or offer to take care of their mother so Mary could go somewhere, but they cared too much for their mother to allow her to be put in a nursing home. Mary never left the house except to go to church. What a terrible way to live! She even had me shop for her clothes.

I slept in the playroom, a room with windows on three sides and window seats under all the windows. There was no other furniture in the room, except the rollaway bed I slept on and that had to be back in the closet as soon as I got up. I had the weekends off, but, since none of my friends knew where I was, I had no place to go. I shopped for nothing in particular on Saturdays and watched the old lady so the family could go to church together on Sunday. There really wasn't a lot for me to do during the week, so I started to do the ironing – something Mary hated to do. There was a ton of it, and I never did catch up. I don't think Little Mary ever wore a dress twice.

Since I was due in October, I checked into the home at the beginning of September, 1962.

Most of the other girls in the home were between fourteen and sixteen and way too young and immature to be mothers or even a mother's helper. They had been put there by their parents, and keeping their babies was not an option. Most really wanted to keep their babies but their parents had the final say. It was such a sad and confusing time for all of us. The only older girl (my age) while I was there was Daisy. When I entered the Home, I had to choose a new name using my initials, JD – for secrecy reasons. Daisy said her real name was Donna.

"You can call me *Jane Doe*," I said.

"No, you can't use that name."

I thought I was really dumb – probably everyone had wanted that name, and it was already used, but no. No one had ever asked for that name and the nuns wouldn't let anyone use such a name. So I was Jane Day.

The Home was in a residential neighborhood a few blocks behind the old Montgomery Wards' store on University Avenue in St. Paul. From the outside of the home, it looked like all the surrounding large upper middle-class homes. Inside the Home it was very much an institution with the left side of the first floor containing offices, sleeping quarters for the nuns, with a nursery in the back. To the right was the chapel. Mass was every morning at seven. Upstairs was a large dorm room with rows of beds, a "sick" room, a large bathroom with several stalls and showers, a sitting room with several tables and chairs, and a craft closet full of donated fabric scraps, threads, etc. In the basement was the large kitchen/dining room. The tables were picnic benches. Behind the building stood the two-story laundry building. Machinery took up the whole first floor and ran the laundry equipment on the second floor. It was probably a converted garage. Access to the laundry was by way of an outside staircase. The laundry room contained two large vats of boiling water on open flames and a vat of disinfectant rinse. Girls would use wooden paddles to stir the clothes and diapers in the vat of wash water then use the paddles to fish them out, feed them through the ringer into the rinse water, then through another ringer into the disinfectant rinse, then one more wringer and into a basket. The wash was then taken outside and hung on clothes lines. The dry clothes and diapers would return to the upstairs laundry to be folded on large tables (this was the job I did when the laundry was short-handed). But my primary job was mopping the bathroom and cleaning the sinks and toilets daily.

Because I was not Catholic, I got special treatment. I had my own room, the sick room. Since no one was sick, the room was empty. During my first two nights I cried myself to sleep, feeling like I had been put in prison for a crime I didn't commit. I was glad I had my own room so no one would know how weak I really was. I thought about Mother and how she must have felt when she arrived at the mental hospital – and she had no idea how long she would be there – unlike me who only had to be here for six weeks. She had to become strong in order to survive for fifteen years. I could be too.

Attendance at mass was required for all the other girls every morning at seven. I didn't have to go since I wasn't Catholic, but sometimes I went anyway. I wasn't impressed. One sweet, tiny old nun sought me out every day to tell me she was praying for me (presumably to convert and see the wisdom of giving my baby to a good Catholic family). I wonder if she felt bad when her prayers weren't answered. We were told our childbirth would be "natural" with no pain relief because they wanted us to remember how painful it was so we would understand the gravity of our sin and maybe save us from making the same mistake twice.

Just before entering the home I called Dad to tell him what I was doing. Surprisingly, he wanted me to come home.

"You need to come home right away and not go into that place. I don't trust them to give you your baby."

"No, I've come this far. They can't keep the baby unless I sign it over."

So, Dad insisted I come home with my baby until I got on my feet and since I really didn't know what I was going to do next, I was grateful.

When Jane was about a month old, I decided it was time for Jerry to take some responsibility so I called him, but he wouldn't take my calls.

Finally, his mother said, "Jerry doesn't want to talk to you so don't call here anymore."

"I want to discuss our daughter. Tell him to call me."

First, they offered to pay for my college if I would put Jane up for adoption and maybe Jerry and I could get back together when he graduated from college. Then they said they'd claim I was an unfit mother and see to it that Jane would be taken away from me.

Before I became pregnant and before I had nixed a future with Jerry, I attended classes to learn about the Catholic Church. They were held at the church on 5th Street, near the U of M campus. After Jane was born, I went back to talk to Father Wilhelm. He suggested Jerry and I have a meeting with him at the church. He arranged it. When I got to the meeting, Jerry was not there but his parents were.

They said, "Jerry was busy studying so we came in his place."

Mmm. Studying in art school.

Lester (Jerry's dad) said, "Jerry doesn't think the baby is his. You're promiscuous and Jerry's friends will testify to that."

I said nothing – I didn't know what *promiscuous* meant and needed to go home and look it up in the dictionary. Although I wasn't sure what it meant, I knew all of Jerry's friends and they were my friends longer than they were his friends. Whatever they said, I knew they wouldn't lie for Jerry.

Connie (Jerry's mother) said, "I'm sure you wouldn't have gotten into this mess if you had had a mother to advise you. I'd like to take the place of your mother and help you through this."

Yet another woman that "wanted" to be my mother. I couldn't think of a single response. Here I was, 21, and people still thought I needed a mother. I thought those days were over. Father Wilhelm seemed to be on their side, believing them, not me, maybe because I gave no defense for myself and I just assumed the priest would be in my corner. Or maybe he thought Catholics would never lie to a priest but a non-Catholic, promiscuous girl might. Anyway, we left with nothing settled except that I was promiscuous. I needed to get home and look it up.

As we were walking to our cars, Lester called out to me, "Well, ha ha, too bad you couldn't keep your pants on." Now, sixty years later, that still stings. Lester and Connie are dead. I'm sure Father Wilhelm is too. That leaves only me to remember.

About a week later, Connie called and asked me to come to their home because Jerry wanted to talk to me. I went and sat in the living room with Jerry for about half-an-hour. He gave me painful looks but couldn't/wouldn't say a word. I finally got up and left, never knowing what he could possibly have wanted to say to me.

His parents' parting words were, "You're ruining three lives."

Then I went to court and had him adjudicated as Jane's father. He had to pay $10.00 a month child support, which I'm sure his parents paid. Maybe I did ruin his life. I hope so. As for me and Jane, we're doing just fine.

| 47 |

A New Start

I called some of my friends and gave them an update on my life. Betty was actually happy and excited for me. I was still living at home and looking for a job.

Finally, I called Jim and we started dating, but I was a different person when I was with him. I was a shrew, and I couldn't seem to stop taking all my anger out on him. Jim's mother, Charlotte, babysat for me when we went out. I was glad to see his mother again, and she had always hoped we would all be a family. Jim was usually on his way to getting drunk when he picked us up. Clearly, he was an alcoholic like the rest of the men in his family.

One time when we were dropping Jane off at Charlotte's and Jane was crying, Jim said, "Just let her cry. She's just spoiled, and you need to ignore her and let her cry." She was three months old.

This time I waited until he brought us home to tell him, "Don't ever call me again."

The hardest part of being a single mom and being the child of a single mom was having no one to share the special moments with. They need to be shared. Your baby needs to hear you brag about her latest conquest/cuteness. I wanted to tell everyone, and I still do – so let me tell you a few things about my amazing daughter, Jane.

Jane, right from the beginning, woke up smiling. I'd tickle her tummy and say, "Tickle tickle," every morning when I got her up.

When Jane was just 6 weeks old, she said her first words! "Lickle lickle," when I leaned over her crib one morning.

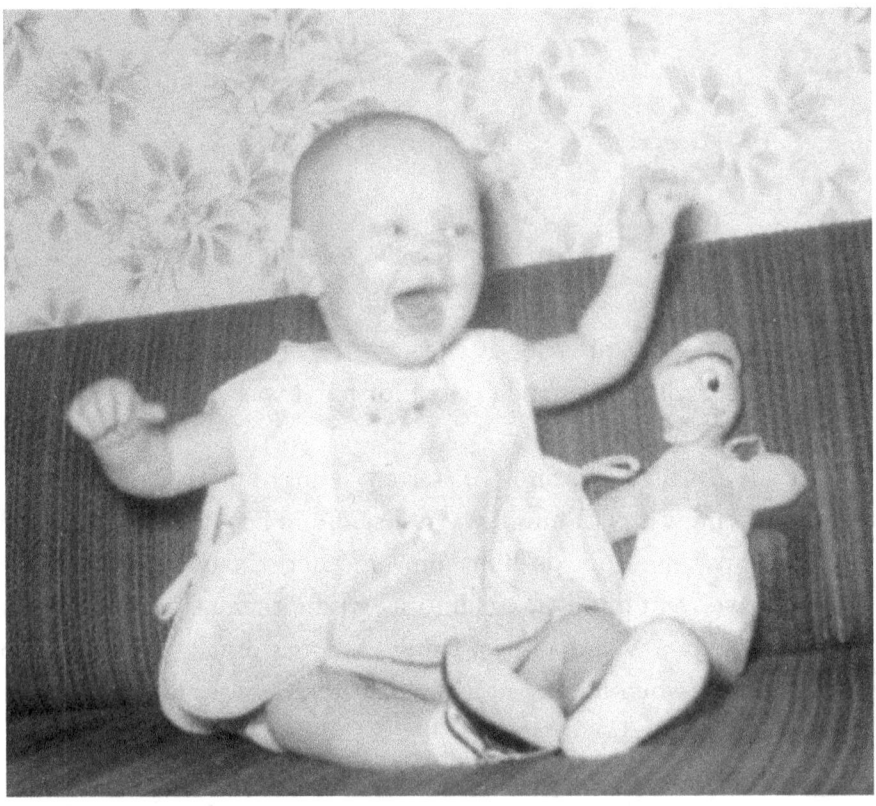

By the time she was one, she was stringing words together, and she never stopped talking. Jane was tiny for her age. When we'd grocery shop, people would have to take a second look when they saw who was talking.

Jane was potty trained before she could walk. I can thank her babysitter, Auntie, for that.

She said, "The first time they sleep through the night without wetting, they are ready to be potty trained."

Jane could read when she was three. I can thank Tony for that. Tony was the other child that Auntie watched. When he started kindergarten, he'd come home to teach Jane everything he had just learned.

I had no social life. I didn't have anything in common with my old friends and when they'd call, I couldn't think of anything to say. Before long, they stopped calling – everyone but Betty. I can see now that I was suffering from depression. Betty wouldn't give up on me. She insisted on dragging me out with friends on Fridays to go bar hopping. Gradually I found things to laugh about with my friends. I will always be grateful to Betty for not giving up on me.

One Friday, at the CC Tap, a guy asked me to dance.

"I don't dance but my friend, Judi, does. Why don't you ask her?"

He did and they eventually got married. But things were never the same between Judi and me after that. I think she put some value on the fact that she was his second choice.

| 48 |

Free At Last - Sort Of

A few years after Mother and Dad's divorce, new laws were enacted in Minnesota and a person that was not deemed mentally ill did not need a guardian to be released. A system of half-way houses was set up to accommodate the newly released patients, and the hospitals were almost emptied. It was a slow process, though, and it was several years before Mother finally had her chance to be released.

I went and picked Mother up to bring her to her halfway house in Minneapolis. I signed the release papers and had *the talk* with Dr. Grimes, the psychiatrist.

He said, "We will probably never know what was wrong with your mother."

Nothing, I thought.

The halfway house was a huge, dark, old house facing Loring Park. When we got to the front door, a creepy old woman greeted us. She wasn't like the witch in *Hansel and Gretel* though. She didn't even attempt to smile at us. I could see her with a poison apple in her hand.

"Mildred? I'll show you to your room."

Turning to me she said, "You can't come in. No visitors allowed. And don't bother to wait for her; we're having lunch now."

"Call me when you can," I said to Mother. I should have waited and taken her shopping or something. It was several weeks before she called.

| 49 |

Betty and Tyler

I got a job at Control Data in the accounting department and was looking for a place I could afford (I was paid $285.00 a month). I paid Dad $75.00 for room and board and the babysitter cost $15.00 per week. I cooked dinner every night.

Betty was going through a bad time. She had married her boyfriend, Butch, when she got pregnant, but Butch was an alcoholic. Shortly after she brought Tyler home from the hospital, Butch got drunk and chased her around their apartment with a knife.

"I'm going to kill you both!" he yelled.

Betty left him but had nowhere satisfactory to go. They were staying with her brother Gary's family temporarily.

We decided we'd find a place together, but it wasn't that easy. No one wanted to rent to single mothers. I heard that a woman I worked with (Dorcy) had a two bedroom upper duplex for rent. At first, she didn't want to rent to us but I begged and pleaded and promised we'd keep the place clean and always pay the rent. And no men moving in. Finally Dorcy relented.

Betty worked nights at Honeywell, and I worked days at Control Data so there were only a couple of hours where we needed a babysitter. This was such a good time for all four of us. I got Jane and Tyler up and fed them breakfast, then went to work. Betty fixed them lunch and entertained them all day. I fixed supper and put them to bed.

I love hot dishes, so that's what I usually made for supper. Once I fixed Spanish rice, which I liked but Jane didn't. When she wouldn't eat it, I told her she had to sit there until she ate at least half her food.

After about fifteen minutes, she said, "I'm done."

I went into the kitchen to look and her plate was clean. I was impressed.

Then she said, "If you find some Spanish rice in the trash, it's because a giant came in and threw it away."

I looked, and sure enough, he had. I didn't fix Spanish rice very often after that.

Mother appeared on a local TV quiz show one Saturday.

She said, "I want to say 'Hi' to my grandson, Ronnie, and my granddaughter, Jane ..."

Before she could finish, Jane yelled at the TV, "Gramma, don't forget Tyler!"

Mother finished, "and Tyler."

One Saturday, when Jane and I went to the laundromat, I saw Clarence sitting on the bench outside the laundromat. He looked terrible. He was super thin and had sores all over his face. We both pretended we didn't know each other. Perfect was over. He didn't want me to see he was an addict, and I didn't want him to know I was an unwed mother.

Betty wanted to move far away, maybe Boston she thought. I decided I had to move far from home too, before Jane started school. In Minneapolis she'd be going to school with children of my high school classmates. I never wanted her to be told she wasn't welcome in another child's home because of what her mother was (promiscuous). Since one of us would need a job right away, I asked my boss, Duane, to find me a job at another location with Control Data. He found me a job in Rockville, Maryland. Of course, because I was a woman, Control Data wouldn't pay any of my expenses or give me a raise, but at least I got the job. My Aunt Babe lived in Arlington, Virginia, so I flew out there (my first ever airplane flight) and stayed with her. She helped me find an apartment near the office. I left Jane with Dad and Margaret and called home every night to see how Jane was. This was the first time we were apart.

'She's doing just fine. We're having a great time."

I wasn't. I had trouble sleeping at night.

Alas, Betty met a guy and decided she didn't want to move after all. I still thought it was best for Jane and me, so I rented the biggest U-Haul available. I loaded all our worldly possessions into the trailer. As big as it was, I still had to leave behind my hats and some furniture.

| 50 |

Road Trip

My brother, Steve, still in high school, and two of his friends offered to help Jane and me move to my new job in Rockville, Maryland. That way they could visit Washington D.C. and have a place to stay. One of his friend's dads worked for an airline and got them return tickets to fly home.

I owned an old 1960, 6-cylinder, rust colored, Chevy Bel Air.

As we were piling into the car to leave, Steve said, "Are you sure this car will pull that big trailer?"

"I guess we're about to find out."

Just like a train, it pulled slowly away from the curb and we were on our way. Minneapolis to Rockville is about sixteen hundred miles and through the Pennsylvania mountains. We planned to drive straight through. No money for hotels.

The boy living in our lower duplex gave Jane two plastic horses as a going away present so for two days and nights, she ran her plastic horses back and forth across the dash, going "ehh, ehh, ehh" (horse whinnies). I don't think she ever slept.

By the time we got near the top of the biggest mountain in Pennsylvania, we were going two miles per hour. There was a mile of traffic behind us, and we were trying to figure out how we were going to back down the mountain when the car finally stopped altogether.

Just in time, we reached the top! We made it! When we finally arrived at our apartment, Steve and his friends rolled out of the car and jumped around on all fours in the grass whinnying like horses.

It had been a long, hard road I'd chosen for Jane and me, but now a heavy burden was lifted and the world was full of happy possibilities! Together Jane and I embarked on our great new adventure as a "divorcee" and her daughter.

| 51 |

Settling In

Most of the women I worked with were divorced mothers and I told them I was divorced too. After all, I came all this way to leave the past behind. I enrolled Jane in school and found a babysitter on the bulletin board in the complex office. The school was located on the grounds of our apartment complex, so Jane could walk across the lawn to school and the babysitter. The new babysitter and her family were from Puerto Rico and her husband worked for the Puerto Rican embassy. Once when I picked her up, no one was home. I was alarmed.

"Were you here all by yourself?"

"No, Pappy's leg was here on the couch with me. We watched TV."

Pappy had a wooden leg and was asleep in the bedroom. I guess a part of a person is as good as a whole one when you're watching TV.

That first Christmas, Jane said one of her friends told her there was no such thing as Santa Claus and she asked me if that was true.

"Well, what do you think?"

After thinking about it for a while she said, "If there was no Santa Claus, then why did God make reindeer that could fly?" I agreed.

On Christmas day, Jane noticed that Santa used the same wrapping paper that we did! That didn't happen again, but the magic was fading.

Jane and I went to visit Babe in Arlington several times. Babe worked at the U.S. Department of Agriculture and had a part-time job working solo at a pizza restaurant Friday and Saturday nights. When visiting her at the pizza restaurant, Babe got a call that her roommate Ellie was in an accident. She wanted me to work the restaurant while she was gone.

"There's nothing to it. Most orders are just pick-ups. Just write down what they want and put it on the pizza. Put it in the oven for 15 minutes, cut it and box it. Here's the menu. Charge what it shows. If they order a Special, put everything on it. Bye."

Sure enough, someone ordered a Special so I put a lot of everything on the pizza. One of the bins contained anchovies but there weren't very many in the bin so I put them all on the pizza. When the man came to pick up his pizza, he was very drunk and had trouble walking. He staggered out, sniffing the air and looking around wondering where that smell was coming from. I hope he enjoyed his pizza.

When Babe came back to close up, I said, "We're out of anchovies. There was only enough for one Special pizza."

Babe laughed, "That was a new can of anchovies and we can put anchovies on ten pizzas with one can. Plus, we only put anchovies on pizzas as a special request. That guy was probably one of my regulars. I can't wait to hear what he has to say about that pizza."

I had to have my rusty 1960 Chevy Bel Aire inspected before I could register the car in Maryland. This was a surprise because there were no inspections in Minnesota. Not only was it all rusty, but I had put a long crack on the big, wraparound windshield when I was trying to remove ice from it. My co-workers said it would never pass inspection with that crack running across the windshield and told me about a place where I could get the sticker for a little extra money. So I did.

Even there, the mechanic said, "Mechanically, this car passes inspection but the whole body fails and should be replaced. Lucky for you, the body is not part of the inspection."

Then I was in an accident that wasn't my fault so I got the windshield fixed. Shortly after that, my brake line broke and I ran into a pickup. The cost to fix it was more than the car was worth (about $100.00). So I bought a car from my boss. It was a 1963 Falcon convertible. I loved that car. But the top was coming apart. I bought a replacement top from the Sears catalog and went down to Babe's so she could help me replace it. It was harder than we thought it would be. The English-as-a-second-language instructions left us guessing and our basic set of tools was inadequate. We discovered we needed things like a socket wrench with a bendable handle and several other unfamiliar tools, so we had to stop working all the time and ask the neighbors if they could loan the necessary tools to us. Some of the neighbors came over to watch and Jane took pictures.

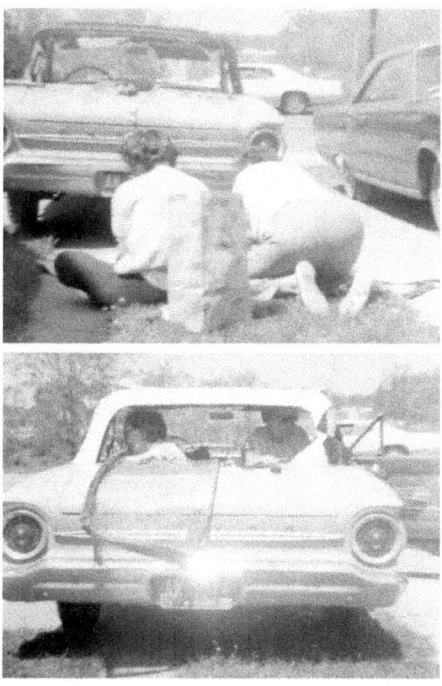

| 52 |

Not a Dog

More than anything, Jane wanted a dog. In kindergarten, I made her a dog costume for Halloween. She loved being a dog and wore the feet out of her dog costume wearing it around the apartment, running on all fours and barking. Of course, this aggravated our neighbors below to no end, and they'd bang on the ceiling and yell at us and threaten to call the office and have us moved or evicted. But Jane went to bed at seven, so I ignored them.

Apparently, they finally called the office, and when the office called, I said, "It's just the two of us. How much noise can my five-year-old daughter and I possibly be making? They must be overly sensitive to noise. Maybe they should move to an apartment on the top floor."

The office suggested I get rugs, but I already had a rug in the living room and didn't think I needed them elsewhere. I think those neighbors eventually moved because they stopped complaining even though Jane was still a dog.

Our apartment complex didn't allow dogs. Plus, we didn't have the time to spend with a dog and train it, so I promised Jane we'd get a dog as soon as we lived in a house. In the meantime, everyone knew Jane wanted a dog, and I guess everyone thought any pet would do.

On Jane's sixth birthday, Alice, a woman I worked with, gave her a parakeet, Christopher. He had flown into the office window of Alice's daughter who gave him to Alice who gave him to Jane for her birthday.

Christopher could talk and would say, "Hello, my name is Christopher."

He'd laugh just like Alice and would repeat any sounds, words or phrases we used repeatedly. He'd eat with us at night, running around the table, sampling everything on our plates. If I had a beer, he'd want to sit on the rim and drink it. I'd only let him have one drink and then cover my glass with my hand. He didn't like that one bit and would squawk at me and peck my hand. Christopher was a lot of fun and a great pet – but still not a dog.

One day Jane and her friend, Bonnie, caught a wild baby rabbit. I put it on the patio in an open box while we looked for a shoe box to put it in, but as soon as at it could, it jumped off the patio! I mistakenly thought it would know better. Down it sailed, three whole stories. We ran down and it was lying on the ground, unconscious. We rushed it to the vet, and she said it was okay, no broken bones or anything.

The vet told the girls, "Wild animals don't make good pets, especially wild rabbits. They almost always die after a few days in captivity, they're so scared."

We kept it for a few days, until I convinced the girls they had to let it go. They took it back to where they found it, close to the woods behind the apartment, and let it go, hoping it would find its mother.

Then, the neighbor kids who lived on the second floor gave Jane a mouse. She named it Nancy. Their father worked in a research lab, and he brought the mouse home from the lab. The kids asked Jane if she wanted it and of course she did. It came in a little plastic lab container. So we bought her a nice cage.

Nancy was a rejected lab mouse because she had a skin condition and had a big scab on her back. When the scab wouldn't go away, the vet suggested I put rubbing alcohol on it. Nancy bit me so the scab remained. When I tried to give her back, the family had moved back to India so Nancy stayed. Nancy was almost blind and was nervous about being out of her cage. Jane was getting Nancy a little comfortable being out in the room until Huey accidentally stepped on her. Nancy screamed and Huey cried, "I'm sorry, I'm sorry." Huey was a new neighbor child, about a year younger than Jane. His father worked for the British Embassy, and they had moved into the same apartment vacated by Nancy's previous owners. Huey was overweight, shy, clumsy, and awkward. He was jumping around, pretending to be afraid. He scared Nancy and she ran right under one of his feet. I don't know who needed more consoling – Huey or Nancy. Fortunately Nancy didn't seem to be hurt, but she wouldn't come out of her cage after that. I feel bad that we never found anything that would make her life happier; she was always afraid.

Then, at Easter, I bought Jane a rabbit because I knew she was sad about giving up the wild rabbit. She named her Fuzzy. We set up a litter box for her in the bedroom and as soon as Jane got home after work, out came Christopher and out came Fuzzy. Nancy stayed in her cage. Fuzzy loved to play *hide under the blanket* with Jane, and she chewed off all the rubber fingers and faces on Jane's dolls. She'd follow me around the apartment and chew on my flip-flops whenever I'd stop walking. They kept getting smaller and smaller until I'd have to buy a new pair. She chewed off the side of the rubber bath mat. Fuzzy was great about using her litter box, except when she was finished, she'd send litter flying all over the bedroom. I kept getting higher and higher boxes but she sent that litter flying straight up and out. We spent a lot of time sweeping. Fuzzy was a great pet – but still not a dog.

Now we had Jane running through the apartment on all fours and barking with Fuzzy hopping at her side and Christopher flying overhead, also barking. And poor little Nancy cowered in the corner of her cage, scared by all the commotion.

Pets make life just a little funner. But a bird and a mouse and a rabbit still don't add up to a dog.

| 53 |

Mother's Visits

Jane and I looked forward to Mother's visits. I loved having her to talk to. Jane loved her visits because she didn't have to go to a babysitter after school, and Mother was happy to take care of Jane. Mother loved playing games with her grandchildren and when Jane was very young, they played Chutes and Ladders, Old Maid, and Go to the Dump. By the time she was in kindergarten, they were into Chinese checkers, Sorry, and Rummy. Mother never let Jane win. She had to earn it. Jane learned she could do anything, even beat Grandma, as long as she tried hard enough. Over the years they moved to more and more complex games like Five Card Draw and Monopoly and 500. Later, when Trivial Pursuit became popular, I always graciously volunteered to let Mother be my partner, especially if someone new was playing with us. We tromped them every time! Mother had an incredible memory for trivia and the past. She was like an encyclopedia.

Jane and I benefitted from her visits because she helped me be a better mother. Once, when I came home from work, I said, "Why did you let Jane go out and play in shorts and a tee shirt? It's winter!"

"She's smart. If she's cold, she'll come in and put on something warm."

On her annual Christmas visit, when Jane was in first grade, Mother brought her giant suitcase that her friend, Casper, had given her. He was a friend from their years in St. Peter State Hospital.

The suitcase was huge, about the size of a steamer trunk, and could hold at least 100 pounds of clothes. Of course, Mother always packed her suitcase after the person taking her to the airport arrived. They would throw in everything close at hand until the suitcase was full and head for the airport. Luckily, back then, the airlines were not so concerned about the weight of suitcases.

Linda worked for TWA and would get Mother stand-by passes to come and visit. I'd wait for her call before I drove to the airport to pick her up since we were never sure what flight she'd come in on. On this one particular visit, our phone wasn't working. It would ring but when I picked up the phone it wouldn't connect. It just kept ringing. Fuzzy had chewed through just enough of the cord that it would ring but not answer, and we couldn't call out. After a few calls, we decided it must be Mother and went to the airport to find her.

Sure enough, she was waiting outside without her suitcase. She couldn't lift it. We checked the luggage turnstile, but, by then, it had disappeared. We finally found it sitting on a rack with other unclaimed luggage and dragged it home and up three flights of stairs.

When she opened it, she said, "Who put all these Lucky Strikes in my suitcase? I don't smoke Lucky Strikes!" *Whoever did this should have known to put Pall Malls in her suitcase.*

Jane was looking in the suitcase and said, "Gramma, why do you have a GI Joe suit and hat in here?"

Who would have guessed there would be more than one of those behemoth suitcases out there? Without a working phone to call the airline, we had to drag the suitcase back to the airport, hunt down the soldier who was looking for his suitcase, and trade it for Mother's.

On Mother's subsequent visits we looked forward to opening her suitcase to see what surprises we might find.

| 54 |

Clarence for the Last Time

In 1968, when Mother was visiting Jane and me in Rockville, MD, Resurrection City was happening in Washington D.C. Resurrection City, or The Poor People's Campaign, was the Rev. Martin Luther King, Jr.'s last dream.

About three thousand poor, mostly black, people were camping on the National Mall just south of the Reflecting Pool.

Mother, while reading the paper, said, "Didn't you go to school with Clarence B.? Well, it says here that he has been arrested for being in a knife fight over drugs down in Resurrection City."

Maybe I should have tried to bail him out. But then, I had to think of Jane's safety, so probably not. I didn't think Clarence was still that kind, mature man I used to care for. When I was young and in love, I thought Clarence had the world in the palm of his hand. Now I know being a man who is black, even in the North, only means people are afraid of you or hate you. Clarence really had only two choices: be a jock and play a game for the entertainment of others or be a bagger in the grocery store where there would always be someone to say, "I don't want him touching my food." Sadly, he chose door number three, be an addict.

In 1983, Clarence was shot to death in Minneapolis, supposedly while trying to rob a dentist. As far as I can tell, it was never investigated, and it turns out the dentist that killed Clarence happened to have been Betty's dentist. Betty said she never knew her dentist had shot Clarence, but she knew her dentist shot and killed his wife. It seems Clarence was just target practice. Such a tragic waste of a beautiful person.

| 55 |

Jerry for the Last Time

Jerry went on to get an MFA in printmaking, got married, and started teaching second grade in Florida, or so his parents told Social Services when I asked for a raise in child support (from $10.00 per month). He couldn't possibly pay more, what with payments on a new car and moving expenses and a new wife.

Curious about what happened to Jerry, in 2003, I found him on the internet and contacted him for the first time since visiting him at his parents' house in 1962. He said he has been married four times, and his current wife was a keeper. He never had kids because he never wanted them, lives in the woods in Oregon without air conditioning and chops firewood for his heat. He paints decorative oars for a living. He said he refuses to speak with any of his family although his sister, Jean, still tries to contact him. He never asked about Jane.

Jane found a couple of her cousins on 23andMe. They thought he lived in California and had heard rumors that he had a child. When Jane told them where he lived, they contacted him.

Jerry - Christmas 1961

After the fires in Oregon in 2020, Jane's cousins said the fires had destroyed all his possessions and property, and he and his wife were only able to save two cats and a dog. At least he loves animals.

| 56 |

Mother

From the time I was a baby until Mother was taken away, she read fairy tales to us every night. The book she read most was *A Child's Book of Famous Stories.* We went to sleep dreaming of all the things possible in our future – scary and yet wonderful. All stories have a happy ending. I still have the book.

Mother was always an avid reader and preferred biographies and memoirs. When Mother was finally released, and whenever she came to visit me, she told me stories - stories of her experiences and the stories of her relatives and friends, some of which I have recounted in this book. I only wish I had recorded them so I could accurately retell all of them.

Mother stayed in Minneapolis so she could be close to her family. Once Grandpa told her she should run away with her boyfriend from St. Peter, Floyd. Floyd intended to move to Denver when he ran away so they could marry. Since neither could be legally released (neither had a guardian willing to take responsibility for them), they couldn't marry in Minnesota. If they applied for a license, they would both be found and returned to the state hospital.

Mother told Grandpa, "I'm not moving that far away. I'll never see my kids."

Linda, Mother, and Jane

Once we (her children) were grown and established enough to have Mother live with us, (by then, I was married and living in Texas) she said, "No." After spending fifteen years having every aspect of her life controlled in state mental hospitals and then having to spend years in half-way houses having everything she did scrutinized, she wouldn't give up her long-fought-for freedom. For me, I finally had my mother back, even if only for short periods of time. She was fun and funny and a great storyteller. And I knew she loved me and thought I could do anything. Mother taught me humor, kindness, empathy, and love are always available to give and receive. And these are the worthwhile things that will make a person happy. My time with her was never enough.

While Mother's life was not the life she wanted or deserved, she was able to accept it and be happy. What more could anyone want?

Mother died at ninety-one, in 2005.

| 57 |

Dad

I went with Dad to his final doctor's appointment when he was 95. His doctor told him all his systems were failing and it was time to put him in hospice. He would probably not live for another six months.

While we waited for Metro Mobility to pick us up, Dad said, "I'm ready to go." Then he asked, "Do you believe in God?"

"No," I said.

"Neither do I."

Dad's life had not gone the way he had aspired. He dreamed of being a photographer and an inventor. He wanted to be involved in the emerging flight industry. Instead, he worked in the best paying job he could find in order to provide the best he could for his family. He started out as a machinist. He went to night school and eventually worked up to become a tool and die maker. I suppose he blamed Mother for subverting his dreams, and, because I was so much like her, I was the constant reminder of all that was lost.

After that last visit to the doctor, he lived on in hospice care for almost three more years. I believe those years were happy years for him. Two of his three daughters and his son told him often how much they loved him and appreciated all that he had sacrificed for them and credited him with molding them into the persons they had become. I couldn't bring myself to say those things. I should have and regret not doing so. Dad left this world knowing he was loved and the sacrifices he made were worth it.

Near the end, he finally told me I was pretty (the only compliment he ever gave me). I don't know what motivated him to say that. I had long ago ceased being upset with him for the way he treated Mother and me because he was a wonderful grandfather, especially to Jane. If only he could have been so free with his affection for his children. But I still couldn't sing his praises.

Shortly before he died, Dad said to me, "I don't think I ever loved your mother, but she gave me four wonderful children."

I was so angry, but as usual, I kept it inside. *She didn't **give** you anyone. You took us from her.* Why would he tell me that, the only one that would be hurt by it? I felt he just had to hurt me one last time. How could he think it was okay to make life-altering decisions for someone he didn't even love? I don't know if I will ever finally forgive him for never loving Mother.

Mother died believing he loved her. She told me so. Years before, on the way to Jane's wedding shower, Mother was raving about the latest thing that Dad did to make her angry.

I asked, "Why are you still so mad at Dad?"

"Because I know he still loves me but is too much of a coward to admit it." If I could believe that I might be able to forgive him.

Dad died at ninety-eight, in 2012.

| 58 |

Life Goes On

In 1971, while Jane and I lived in Maryland, I met and married my first husband, Bob. Jane was eight. We lived in Montreal and bought Jane her first dog, Sticker. Three years later, we moved to Texas, Bob's home state. He wanted to come home. In 1976, Bob and I had a son, Steve. Our marriage lasted for nineteen years but sadly we grew apart. Still, those years were full of great stories, and I think I'll write about them in my next book.

I asked Mother why she thought her marriage didn't work out.

She said, "I never should have married your dad. He has no sense of humor."

I realized I've never had a relationship with a man with a good sense of humor, except maybe Clarence. We laughed a lot together. That may be why none of my relationships with men have lasted. I look for the humor in everything. Just as their negativity and view that life is hard and thankless eventually grates on me, my propensity to laugh off setbacks and just move on eventually grates on them. They seem to think I must be stupid and need someone to remind me of my failures.

After all this time, I've finally given up on trying to find a humorous man to enjoy my last years with.

Jane, Steve, and me

My children are kind, loving, and humorous. They happen to be really smart too. They're both happily married to wonderful partners. Jane lives in Atlanta and Steve and I are still in Texas but I hope someday to go home to Minnesota where my core values still live. But no matter where I am, Mother will always be alive in my heart and in my genes and once in a while, I catch a glimpse of her in the mirror - a gesture, a frown, her smile.

| 59 |

The Three-Legged Frog - A Fairytale

Once upon a time, not so very long ago, in a kingdom not so far away, lived a beautiful princess. On warm sunny days she loved to sneak away to a little hidden pond in the woods near the palace and go for a swim. When she would get there, she always looked around to make sure she was alone (for she liked this time by herself). This one particular day, when she was sure she was alone, she took off her robe and dived in. When she came up, she found she had something holding on tight to her hand! It was a three-legged frog, and that frog was hanging on with all five arms and legs.

She tried to shake him loose, but he yelled, "Stop! I'm really a handsome prince and if you will only kiss me, I will turn back into my former self."

The princess looked long and hard at this talking, three-legged frog and finally said, "You really are a special frog – with three legs and all, but I'm not so sure I'd be interested in a three-legged prince".

The princess was also very special for she was smart.

Quickly the frog replied, "I don't REALLY have a third leg. When that wicked witch was turning me into this frog, she whacked me with her magic wand. Just as I was turning into a frog, I grabbed the wand

and it attached itself to me as another leg! If you change me back into a prince, I can use the magic wand to grant your every wish, and we can be married and live together happily ever after."

At this the princess responded, "Being a princess, I already have everything I desire and, frankly, I find it rather boring. Besides, I would never marry someone I picked up in a dive."

With that, she threw him back in the pond and grabbed her robe and went home.

Of course, the frog was extremely upset with this unexpected turn of events. In fact, he was doubly upset because he thought he had figured out the perfect scam and had lied to the princess. The truth is, before he was turned into a frog, he was Farley, the Three-Legged Man in the circus. That "wicked witch" who turned him into the frog was really his mother-in-law, Cassandra, and she was the fortune-teller in the circus. She turned him into a green frog because she was so mad at him for the way he treated her only daughter, Lisa (known as Lizard Lady in the circus). Cassandra, in a fit of anger, put a curse on him, telling him the only way he could get his life back was to find some woman willing to kiss his ugly, slimy green face.

Farley had been pretty smug about his plans. He knew the princess came often to the pond because he used to spy on her when he was a man. All he had to do now was sit and wait. And he thought his story was fool proof. Who, princess or not, would not want everything handed to them – just wish for it and you'd have it. He would have the court tailor make his clothes to hide the third leg with one of his other legs, and, once he was part of the royal family, the princess would never figure out that everything she wished for came from her father, the king, just like before, and not her new husband. It's well known that beautiful princesses are always stupid.

While Farley was sitting on a log, pondering his next move, who should show up at the pond but his wife, Lizard Lady! She slowly waded into the pond, wiggling her webbed toes in the cool mud on the bottom of the pond. When she reached a rock in a sunny spot of the pond, she sat down and began to quietly sob. Big alligator tears ran down her scaly cheeks and splashed in the pond around her.

Farley watched her for a while and began to think of how badly he had treated her for so many years. Lisa had not been Lizard Lady when he married her; she was a beautiful trapeze artist. As time went on, she developed a dry skin problem which made her skin look scaly, and then her skin took on a pale, greenish tinge. Her gorgeous skimpy costumes had to cover more and more of her scaly skin until she looked more like a gymnast in sweats. And it took more and more time to cover her scaly face with heavy make-up. The higher-ups in the circus finally told her they were replacing her with someone prettier. This was a hard time for Lisa, but Farley hadn't been supportive. He felt he had been cheated and was saddled with a toadish wife. Farley had always had a roving eye and now he didn't even bother to try to hide his affairs with other women. Lisa should be grateful to even have a husband.

Lisa and her mother, Cassandra, came up with a plan so she could remain in the circus. Lisa could brush on a light coat of green powder to enhance her scaly skin and then she could wear her skimpy trapeze costumes, after all, she still had a great body. She made a charming Lizard Lady and was a big attraction. Sometimes, as part of Lisa's act, she would eat a sardine. It was a big hit with the audience. Then she thought live goldfish would be even better. They weren't so bad.

Farley still felt cheated and never missed an opportunity to be verbally abusive to Lisa. Lisa still loved Farley and thought their problems were all her fault.

After watching Lisa crying on the rock, Farley, for the first time in his life, felt empathy and realized how much he had hurt Lisa. He thought he could change his ways and give up most of his girlfriends. In fact, maybe he could even give up that new trapeze artist! None of them cared as much for him as Lisa did. Yes, he decided his former life wasn't so bad and he resolved right then and there to be a good husband to Lizard Lady.

He swam seductively toward Lisa and smiled lovingly at her. She saw him through her tears and reached out her hand to him and he swam into it. She brought him close to her face and looked carefully at him through her teary eyes.

"What a sweet frog you are! And you have three legs, just like my husband – but he would never have looked so sweetly at me. He always had a mean look in his eyes," she mused.

Just at the same moment that Farley opened his mouth to speak, Lizard Lady opened her mouth, popped Farley in and swallowed him.

Slowly she rose from her rock and dried her eyes, thinking, "Suddenly I feel SO much better."

NOTES AND REFERENCES

Chapter 1

The stock market crash of 1929 resulted in unemployment tripling to four point five million within sixty days. Nearly one million people took part in hunger marches across the country. By 1938, unemployment rose to almost twenty-six million.

In 1930 the New Deal was enacted, which included the CWA (Civil Works Administration), which employed thousands for civic purposes such as constructing parks, roads, and schools.

Reference:

American Decades 1930 –1939, Edited by Victor Bondi, Gale Research Inc., A Manly, Inc. Book 1995

Chapter 7

In 1942, Psychosurgery, authored by Freeman and Watt, is published. It extolls the amazing results of Freeman's new surgery, the lobotomy, and became an instant hit. Like snake oil, the lobotomy is said to cure everything and especially mental illness. It was embraced by the medical community – unfortunately without any substantiating research.

In the mid 1940's lobotomies were the newly discovered cure for any and all behaviors deemed "abnormal." Thousands were performed before anyone thought to study the long-term effects. Lobotomies were given to veterans who lost limbs in the war to ease their phantom pain, to rebellious children, to women who were angry with their husbands, to children with intellectual disabilities, and to people deemed mentally ill. After studies were finally done and the devastating effects finally uncovered, the practice was stopped. But there was no getting back what was taken from the thousands of anguished and trusting souls.

Mother was taken to the Mayo Clinic for a lobotomy. There was no indication that a written evaluation by a psychiatrist was done, no formal hearing, no input from Mother, just Dad's consultation with doctors at the Mayo Clinic.

No one, including Dad and the medical profession, understood how a lobotomy affected a person. Dad expected her to be the same, hard-working mother and wife with boundless energy that she used to be, but without the anger. No studies concerning the long-term effects of the procedure had been performed.

For Mother's lobotomy, her head was completely shaved and two holes were drilled in the top of her skull, just behind her frontal lobe, about two inches apart. Then the doctors sawed a line between the holes and inserted a knife and ran it back and forth to sever the frontal lobe from the rest of her brain. She was awake during the entire procedure so they could observe her reactions. When she could no longer respond to their questions, their job was done.

Although Mother was essentially catatonic, the doctors put her on tranquillizers in case she was still angry. The next step after a lobotomy was to recuperate in the hospital for two weeks and then be released. The patient was determined cured, so nothing more was required of the hospital.

In 1946, mental hospitals had 700,000 beds (230,000 were substandard) for 1,500,000 patients. 29 mental hospitals had no psychiatrist at all. The MHs were desperate for treatments and shock treatments were instituted. Psychoanalyst Roy Grinker commented, "The busy psychiatrist now hardly waits for the patient to undress in his hospital before shocking them into insensibility."

Unheard by the general public, a Dr. Rioch, an eminent neuroanatomist turned psychiatrist, was disturbed by the permanent destruction of brain tissue during lobotomy procedures. He said that prefrontal lobotomy was a therapy that "amputated functions" and characterized it as "partial euthanasia."

One month after Mother's surgery, a medical report came out detailing the immense toll lobotomies took on the mental abilities of the patient, written by Dr. Rylander, a Swedish investigator who had studied thirty-two lobotomized people.

He stated, "It is a man-made self-destructive procedure that specifically destroys several human functions which have been slowly evolved and that especially separate us from other animals."

"They were shallow and show no depth of feeling."

"They show no evidence of real happiness or real sorrow."

"They forget and lose interest in everyday happenings."

The reality for Mother was that her memories from the recent past had been erased. She didn't know what had happened to her. She didn't even remember giving birth to Steve.

According to Dr Rylander, "They (lobotomized patients) are incapable of associating mentally freely."

Mother could no longer visualize the future, plan ahead or solve problems by extrapolation.

"They have a tendency to perseverate."

Perseveration is often associated with damage to the frontal lobe. It means: having difficulty stopping involuntary repetitive behavior.

"Many lose a sense of value for money."

In 1954, Canadian physicians developed a drug to treat schizophrenic patients, Thorazine. In mental institutions, Thorazine was used indiscriminately on any patient regardless of symptoms. During the 50's, one in three families would admit a member to a mental institution. Fewer people were afflicted with cancer than mental illness, yet cancer received 400% more research money. With the ignorance and neglect of mental illness, mental hospitals became little more than overcrowded warehouses where tormented people waited to die. The average budget for meals in mental institutions was 16¢ per meal per patient. The American Institute of Mental Health allowed that within the first year of confinement, a patient had a 50-50 chance of being released, a 6% chance in the second year, and a 1% chance after that. Drugs were expensive so the preferred form of treatment was EST (electroshock therapy). One patient was documented to have undergone 427 bouts of EST.

References:

Psychosurgery: Intelligence, Emotion & Social Behavior Following Prefrontal Lobotomy for Mental Disorders, Freeman and Watt 1942

This book vastly extended the interest in lobotomy. Freeman claimed that severing the connections between the thinking brain and the feeling brain produces individuals whose emotional reactions are less intellectualized and whose intellectualized reactions are less emotionalized.

Group for the Advancement of Psychiatry, Research on Prefrontal Lobotomy, Quotes from Dr. Rylander, Report No.6 June 1948

Great and Desperate Cures, Elliot S. Valenstein, Basic Books, Inc. 1986

Dr. Gosta Rylander observed that had it not been for the Freeman-Watts book and

their standard lobotomy procedure, he doubted that much would have come of it. In Valenstein's assessment of Freeman's book, he states, "Such ideas, while containing some element of truth, were clearly dangerous in their arrogant oversimplification of very complex processes.

American Decades 1950 – 1959, Edited by Richard Layman, Gale Research Inc., A Manly, Inc. Book 1994

Chapter 8

In the 1940s, The Minnesota Unitarian Church began investigating the national reports of shameful conditions in mental hospitals. By 1947, 83% of the patients in mental hospitals were involuntarily committed by family members. Almost 40% of the patients' infirmities were typical of old age. Most of the senile cases died within six months of admission.

References:

The Great Charity, Wm. D. Erickson, St. Peter Regional Treatment Center 1991

The Crusade for Forgotten Souls, Susan Bartlett Foote, Univ. of Minnesota Press 2018

Chapter 12

In 1909, the White House Conference on the Care of Dependent Children began the introduction of Children's Homes. They were extensively used during the late '20s and early '30s during the depression when many parents were unable to even feed their children. These children were not considered orphans and were not available for adoption but were put in these homes by their parents temporarily until they were able to take care of their children once again. The need for Children's Homes significantly dropped in 1935 when Roosevelt initiated Social Security and grandparents were financially able to help take care of their grandchildren. By the mid 1950's most Children's Homes were closed.

Chapter 24

Many patients died in the state hospitals because they no longer had a guardian or their guardians refused to take them out. Many were not mentally ill, just old and wealthy enough that a relative wanted their money or property. Women who claimed their husbands beat them were admitted to the mental hospitals labeled as 'delusional.' Mother told stories about the elderly that she helped to care for (patients were often enlisted as unpaid helpers) and said their biggest fear was dying in the mental hospital. Sure enough, the hospital graveyard usually became their final resting place. The graves behind the hospital were marked only with a number.

A woman Mother was very fond of had trouble swallowing, so Mother would mash up her food and slowly feed her all her meals. Then Mother came home on one of her many tries at being released. By the time Dad sent her back, the woman had died. She had choked to death while being fed. This memory always brought tears of regret to Mother.

Reference:

The Great Charity, Wm. D. Erickson, St. Peter Regional Treatment Center 1991

Chapter 36

Part of the divorce summons served on Mother. Article 5 states the grounds for divorce (Mental Illness).

```
State of Minnesota,  } ss.         IN PROBATE COURT,
County of  Hennepin  }             Commitment to State Hospital

                   { Mental illness  }
In the matter of the { Senility      } of   Mildred A. Druley
                   { Psychopathic Personality }

       To        The Sheriff of Hennepin County
                 (Here insert Sheriff, Constable, or the name of the person designated by the Court.)

and to the Superintendent of the Rochester State Hospital for the mentally ill at Rochester, Minnesota.
          Mildred A. Druley          having been, upon examination, found to be mentally ill
and a resident of   Minneaplis, Minnesota   County   Hennepin
```

Some of the awards for Dad in the divorce: absolute divorce, care and custody of the minor children, the home and furnishings, did not provide for alimony or support money.

STATE OF MINNESOTA   DISTRICT COURT
COUNTY OF HENNEPIN   FOURTH JUDICIAL DISTRICT

Leslie L. Druley,   )
)
        Plaintiff,   )
)
vs.   )
)   S T I P U L A T I O N
Mildred A. Druley,   )
)
        Defendant.   )

That a Judgment and Decree in the above entitled action was entered on the 16th day of October, 1956, giving and granting to the plaintiff herein an absolute divorce from the defendant, and

WHEREAS, Said judgment and Decree granted the care and custody of the minor children of the parties to the plaintiff and gave and granted to him the home and the furnishings located therein, and

WHEREAS, Said Judgment and Decree did not provide for alimony or support money for the defendant herein, she being at said time in a mental institution, to-wit: The State Hospital at St. Peter, Minnesota, and

WHEREAS, On the Motion of defendant's attorney Arnold I. Feinberg to which is appended defendant's Affidavit in support thereof, both of which are dated the 21st day of May, 1965. An Order to Show Cause was issued by the Honorable Dana Nicholson, one of the Judges of the above named Court, which said Order to Show Cause was returnable on the 9th day of June, 1965, and

WHEREAS, a hearing was had on said 9th day of June, 1965, at which said hearing Arnold I. Feinberg appeared as attorney for the defendant Mildred A. Druley, at which time and place the said Mildred A. Druley was present in person, and Louis J. Moriarty appeared as attorney for Leslie L. Druley and the said Leslie L. Druley appeared in person, and

Chapter 48

Letter from Dr. Grimes giving Mother his excuse for not granting her final release.

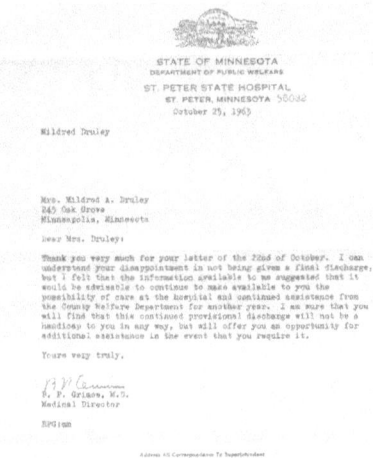

State of Minnesota, Department of Public Welfare St. Peter State Hospital, St. Peter Minnesota 56082 October 25, 1963 Dear Mrs. Druley: Thank you very much for your letter of the 22nd of October. I can understand your disappointment in not being given a final discharge, but I felt that the information available to me suggested that it would be advisable to continue to make available to you the possibility of care at the hospital and continued assistance from the county Welfare Department for another year. I am sure that you will find that this continued provisional discharge will not be a handicap to you in any way, but will offer you an opportunity for additional assistance in the event that you require it. Yours very truly, B. P. Grimes, MD, Medical Director

Copyright © 2022 by Jan Ellis

All rights reserved. No part of this book may be reproduced in any manner whatsoever without written permission except in the case of brief quotations embodied in critical articles and reviews.

First Printing, 2022

www.ingramcontent.com/pod-product-compliance
Lightning Source LLC
LaVergne TN
LVHW021814060526
838201LV00058B/3387